About the screenplay

I've been writing for many years now and a Civil War buff since I saw **The Undefeated** with John Wayne as a kid (*"Conversation kinda' dried up, ma'am."*).

Like the North and South, it was inevitable that my two sides would also collide one day. That happened after reading about Mosby's exploits, which seemed like a movie that I wanted to see on the big screen. I had never written a screenplay and thought the format would be a new challenge, but surely not as hard as writing my novel.

I was dead wrong. A screenplay is completely visual and has to be tighter than Scrooge's purse strings because the whole story must be done in less than 120 pages! It is a very hard task to do well.

After I finished writing **Something Gray**, I had some very high praise from professional actors, directors, screenwriters, and agents, but always with the same refrain. *"Hollywood won't make a Period Piece unless your name is Hanks, Howard, or Spielberg. Write something else."* How discouraging to work so hard for naught.

But they were right. Hollywood is a business first and foremost, and the elite mostly ignored my queries. So I figured I'd try some of the screenplay contests to get noticed.

Something Gray finished in the top 10-15% in three of the major contests of 2012, which was very encouraging since some had almost 8,000 entries, but despite that mild success even a notable script can get buried in the thousands and thousands of screenplays piled up in Los Angeles every year. It's hard to even get yours read, let alone sold. So should I just stick this in a drawer and move on? Sure seemed like it. I was a tad discouraged and started working on other projects.

After I finished my novel, **Xposure**, I ran across Dave Trottier's article on publishing your screenplay as an e-book for Kindle, and figured what the heck? So for all the folks who asked to read all of it (the first 15 pages were temporarily available at www.TotallyWriteousCopy.com), here it is in its entirety.

The appearance of a screenplay is very different from what you may be used to in reading a novel. It may take a few scenes for you to get used to "seeing" a movie on paper, but Mosby will draw you in pretty quickly. Two "stage commands" are essential to follow along: V.O. stands for "Voice Over" (the narrator) and O.S. stands for "Off Screen" (we hear them, but we do not see them, per se).

John Singleton Mosby was a fascinating guy and stood up to bullies his whole life. The size of the tyrant, as the Union painfully discovered, made no difference to him. He was always all in, and even after the war showed the same tenacity in standing with the "other side" if he felt it proper, becoming friends with U.S. Grant and even commending Lincoln for freeing the slaves!

A tragic hero of sorts, always fighting someone or some thing, even himself as you'll see here, Mosby was truly one-of-a-kind.

I hope you enjoy his story and that it makes it to the silver screen one day. I'd pay to see this adventure, and as hard as it may be to believe, most of this story is true!

When you finish the story, and only <u>after you've read THE END, look up this link to see the real Sgt Meeks: http://bit.ly/1aaBNyp</u>.

So let's meet the "Gray Ghost" of the Confederacy, Colonel John Singleton Mosby!

FADE IN:

WHITE WORDS ON A BLACK SCREEN

"We all declare for Liberty; but in using the same word we do not all mean the same thing. With some the word Liberty may mean for each man to do as he pleases with himself, and the product of his labor; while with others the same word may mean for some men to do as they please with other men, and the product of other men's labor.

Here are two, not only different, but incompatible things, called by the same name-Liberty. And it follows that each of the things is, by the respective parties, called by two different and incompatible names-Liberty and Tyranny."

-Abraham Lincoln

EXT. CALIFORNIA BEACH - DAY

SUPER: SANTA MONICA, CALIFORNIA, 1896

MOSBY (63), sits in the sand. A jack-knife, small, sharp, and scrappy, he sports a black suit, extra starch, no jacket.

>   AARON (V.O.)
> Heard tell, truth gets dressed up by
> them who wins a war, less your own
> eyes give it a Saturday night scrub,
> maybe so. Now this here's Sabbath
> square, leastwise mostly so, course
> my recollectin' ain't what it was.

Sand mounds, lined with rows of shells and pebbles, in crisp military formation, offer battle to Mosby's shark-eyed glare.

>   AARON (V.O.)
> No more'n two eyes an' a wiggle when
> I first seen John Singleton Mosby.

An undersized boy in short pants, GEORGIE (10), opposes him. A wallflower with no water or sun, and maggot pale; smaller kids take a sock at him just to feel good about themselves.

>   AARON (V.O.)
> Well sir, I s'pose most figgered me
> just his slave, but them who rode
> with the 43rd knew how it cut.

Two horses graze behind the looming battle. Ivory handled Colt revolvers rest on Mosby's folded jacket.

                    AARON (V.O.)
          We'd a whooped 'ol Billy Yank sure,
          ifn' Bobby Lee fought like I done
          taught the Colonel. Our fightin'
          woulda' warmed an Egyptian mummy.

Mosby notices Georgie approach, stiffens, and snaps a salute.

                    MOSBY
          The troops are formed, General Lee.

Georgie returns the salute, moves toward Mosby, and stares
down at the pistols.

                    GEORGIE
          Colonel Mosby, you ever get scared?
          Of dying, I mean.

                    MOSBY
          Never seen a brave man, son. All
          men are frightened. It's the Beast.

                    GEORGIE
          The Beast?

                    MOSBY
          That belly sick, make ya' spit your
          guts up, and run home to mama feeling?
          Fear, Georgie, is a beast. One you
          best collar, sooner the better.

Mosby stands and puts his hands on Georgie's shoulders.

                    GEORGIE
          You just funning me, Colonel?

                    MOSBY
          Get licked much? The truth, now.

                    GEORGIE
          Well, some boys at school-

                    MOSBY
          Thought so. About your age when a
          friend educated me about the Beast.

                    GEORGIE
          Real, so you can see him?

                    MOSBY
          Feel him mostly. Like 'ol Scratch.
          Never stops prowling. Never sleeps.
          Never chooses sides.

                              GEORGIE
                    Some boys at school say we was on
                    the wrong side. That your Rangers
                    were horse thieves and such. That-

                              MOSBY
                    Ah, s'all bosh! Why, every horse we
                    took had an armed Yank in the saddle.

                              GEORGIE
                    So you didn't ride with any bad men?

                              MOSBY
                    Only one man ever give me cause.

Mosby picks up his Colts. Georgie's eyes track their flight.

                              MOSBY
                    Face still jiggers me time to time.

He notes the boy's fascination with his pistols.

                              GEORGIE
                    Musta' been some face.

                              MOSBY
                    Well son, you don't forget a face
                    that needed that Colt emptied in it.

EXT. COUNTRY ROAD - MORNING

SUPER: FRY'S WOODS, VIRGINIA, 53 YEARS PRIOR

Two boys plod a dusty road, one black and one white. JACK
MOSBY (10), chicken-legged and scrawny, trails the black
boy, ABSALOM (12), who shoulders a large strap of books.

                              ABSALOM
                    Come on, Jacky boy. Keep up.

                              JACK MOSBY
                    I can lug my own books, just so's
                    you know.

                              ABSALOM
                    I'm ta' tote 'em for you, your momma
                    says, on a'counts you so feeble.

                              JACK MOSBY
                    Thunder, Absalom! Makes a man feel
                    like a kitten in a sack.

Mosby kicks a dirt clod and trots up to Absalom.

JACK MOSBY
Well, s'long as you know I can do
it, s'pose it's alright if you tag
along, since you belong to me anyways.

Absalom stops cold and stares, but Mosby keeps walking. The
barb has hooked the fish.

JACK MOSBY
You heard me right. You mine, same
as them books.

ABSALOM
Make sure no harm comes ta' Jacky,
that's what your Mam says. Didn't
say no how to learn you some manners.

JACK MOSBY
I can take care a myself, but I don't
mind much. Considering yer a nigger
and all, I figure we's still friends.

ABSALOM
This nigga'll knock some sense into
your scrawny cotton ass.

Mosby turns and comes back to Absalom. He scrounges in his
pocket and hands him a peace offering.

JACK MOSBY
Here. Know what that is?

ABSALOM
Nothin' but an 'ol smithy nail for a
hoss shoe, 'cept bent up some.

JACK MOSBY
It's a friendship ring. Yo' daddy
made it, when Poppa wasn't around.

ABSALOM
So? What I want it for?

JACK MOSBY
Means we's friends. For life, like
the Three Musketeers. Stand up for
one another. All for one and one
for all.

Absalom softens, slides it on, and admires it.

ABSALOM
Fits purty good. Ain't had no ring
before. Always and for ever?

                    JACK MOSBY
          Always and forever. I got one too.

                    ABSALOM
          What 'bouts bein' your nigga'?

                    JACK MOSBY
          Ah, I'm just playing ya', Abby.

                    ABSALOM
          Mebbe I don't want no friendship
          with you. You ever figger on that?

                    JACK MOSBY
          If you could read, you'd know how
          important it is to have a friend for
          life. Like the Three Musketeers.

                    ABSALOM
          Exactly what is a Muskrat-tear?

                    JACK MOSBY
          They's French sword fighters.

                    ABSALOM
          Real swords?

                    JACK MOSBY
          Absolutely. Stand up for the helpless
          and less fortunate po' folk in Europe.

Mosby stops and studies the road, then brightens.

                    JACK MOSBY
          B'jiminey! Why don't you stay Abby?
          I can show ya' how to sword fight
          come recess.

                    ABSALOM
          Think it'd be aw-right with yer Mam?

                    JACK MOSBY
          Why shore I do. See, we needs each
          other. So long as we stick together,
          ain't nobody ever gonna bully us,
          Absalom. Nobody!

                    ABSALOM
          Okay, Jacky boy. I'll Musketeer
          with you, on your word of honor that
          we stand by each other, no matter.

Mosby crosses his heart and solemnly spits. Arm in arm,
they march toward a small schoolhouse in the distance.

EXT. SCHOOL YARD - AFTERNOON

Recess.

A crowd of white children whoop and holler. At the mob's center, Absalom teeters on a crate, fighting back tears.

                  GEORGE TURPIN
        What'm I bid for this monkey boy?

The pack howls.

                  ABSALOM
        Please Mister Turpin-

                  GEORGE TURPIN
        Shut yer pie hole, nigga'!

GEORGE TURPIN (12), slaps him. Everything about him blubbers fat. Swollen face, grimy neck folds, stubby fingers. When his bulgy lips part, even his teeth look fat.

                  BIDDER ONE
        Five dollars and a three legged hog!

                  GEORGE TURPIN
        I'm bid five and a crippled pig.

                  BIDDER TWO
        Ten dollars an' a blind mule!

                  GEORGE TURPIN
        Kin I git 20 and a jackass?

                  BIDDER ONE
        Ya'll ready got the jackass!

The children laugh louder and he cuffs Absalom again, then stops when he hears...

SILENCE.

The swarm parts. Mosby advances, face to face with Turpin.

                  GEORGE TURPIN
        Speak of the Devil an' he appears.
        Halloo Jack...Ass!

                  JACK MOSBY
        You cannot sell my friend.

Jack clenches his fists and draws back the nail ring hand.

                    GEORGE TURPIN
          Friend? Go on for I squash you like
          a weevil. Seen bigger tits on a bul-

WHACK! WHACK!

Mosby quivers, and then crumples.

Senseless, curled on the ground, Mosby sobs bloody puffs of
dust. He can see Absalom's eyes plead, well up, and gush.

The crowd cinches tighter and Absalom wilts from view.

EXT. MOSBY FARMYARD - EVENING

AARON (45), grooms a large Bay near the barn. The two boys
near. Jack trails Absalom, who no longer carries his books.

Absalom peels off to a small shack behind the barn.

Careful to keep Aaron between him and the massive horse,
Jack drifts in and drops his books.

                    AARON
          'Bout time you young 'uns show'd.
          Yo' Mam 'bout split a gut. Best git
          on in there now.

                    JACK MOSBY
          I'm real sorry Uncle Aaron. We....

He begins to sniffle and then breaks down.

                    AARON
          Now, now. See here. Ain't no cause
          fer carryin' on, Jack. We was jus'
          worried, s'all.

                    JACK MOSBY
          It ain't for being behind my time.
          For letting Absalom git sold off.

                    AARON
          Sold off? Sold off'n by who?

                    JACK MOSBY
          Them boys at school auctioned him
          off at recess. That shit tickler
          Turpin done it!

                    AARON
          Watch yer mouth, boy.

                    JACK MOSBY
          Yes, sir.

AARON
You means to say George Turpin tried to auction off my Abby?

JACK MOSBY
It ain't funny. They sold him to a boy from Five Forks for 40 dollars!

AARON
I's sorry Marse Jack. Don't means to laugh, but them boys ain't sold nobody no how.

JACK MOSBY
They ain't?

AARON
No sir-ree. Them boys ain't got no 40 dollar and they sho' ain't got no auctioneer license.

JACK MOSBY
Ya' think?

AARON
Why sho'. I knows auctions. Wipe yer nose and git ready for supper now. Yo' Momma been a fright worryin' o'er ya'll. I see to Abby.

JACK MOSBY
I tried to stand up. Gave my word, but...just tired a' bein' sickly s'all. Like ta' whoop that Turpin upside his fat cow head!

AARON
'Spect his itch get rubbed soon 'nuff, but mebbe yer time finally come round.

JACK MOSBY
Time? For what, Uncle Aaron?

AARON
The Phil-Oh-Steen Phil-Os-Oh-Fee.

JACK MOSBY
The Phil-a-what? You joshin' me?

AARON
Look here, boy. Yo' Momma loves ya, mebbe too much, but yo' head ain't screwed on right 'bout bein' a man in this world.

Just a stare.

                    AARON
          Sometimes ya' jest can't fight fair!
          Don' much matter if ya wins, ya'
          just gotta stand up to bullies. Use
          fear as a weapon. The Beast, boy.

Mosby looks like he ate sour apples and rubs a bloody trickle.

                    AARON
          Hear me now, child. Hit first, hard
          and fast, see? Unexpected like.
          An' while they's dazed, same as a
          duck hit on a head with a rock, skee-
          daddle. Hit an' git!

Aaron gets more animated, demonstrating footwork, and jabs.
Jack, mesmerized, begins to get it, and grins.

MONTAGE - AARON LEARNS MOSBY UP

                    AARON (V.O.)
          I 'splained the story a' David an'
          the Phil-o-steen giant. How David
          trained for sheep. Jus' him and the
          Lord. How he attacked Go-liath, ran
          right at him and surprised him!

-- Twilight, a groggy Mosby shovels up Aaron's eggs, drinks
some coffee, grimaces, and grabs his shotgun. From the
kitchen window, Absalom watches him walk toward the woods.

-- Afternoon, he returns, tosses a bony, runt rabbit on the
kitchen table where Aaron prepares supper, impressed.

                    AARON (V.O.)
          I teached Jack how David stood up to
          everything, learnt to fight lions
          an' bears. Move fast! Strike first.
          Make the Beast work for you.

-- Mosby's in a school fight, lands the first blow, but ends
up on the bottom taking his licks, again.

-- He comes home, bloodied. Aaron dips a rag at the pump
and dabs his face, while Absalom grimaces at the deep scrapes.

                    AARON (V.O.)
          Lord was teachin' David for Go-liath,
          but Jack was a'fixin' to face his
          own giant. I could see right off,
          Jacky boy had the sand.

-- Wide-eyed, Mosby clenches a horse's neck, and circles the corral, while Aaron holds the rope at center. He falls off and Absalom giggles. Riled, he glares, and mounts up again.

-- The early hunt scene repeats, and he returns with two squirrels and a rabbit...and tries some more coffee.

                    AARON (V.O.)
        If'n you gonna fight, first thump
        best be a thriller. Hit hard soon.
        And never fight fair. Turn fear on
        them, let the Beast chew their hide.

-- The boys laugh in front of a full-length looking glass, comparing Abby's brown skinned eyelids with Mosby's shiners.

-- Mosby rides alone, faster and more agile, as Aaron and Absalom watch astride the corral fence, nodding approvingly.

-- The hunt scene echoes, older and taller, but still gaunt, Mosby drops a turkey on the table, and slurps his coffee.

-- The short end of the stick again, Mosby meets Aaron at the pump with a confident air, and offers Aaron his own rag.

                    AARON (V.O.)
        Put Lord's fear in them first, so
        the Beast git on them. Sides, nobody
        gonna kill ya. Go ahead and fight,
        but hit hard. And move fast!

-- A ruffled Mosby returns without a black eye, and Aaron beams, until he turns his head and presents the purple mouse.

-- Mosby rides across the rich, rolling Virginia countryside, leaps some logs, races a fox, and charges up steep bluffs. Aaron and Absalom wave as he tops the far hill, rearing up.

-- Skunked, a teenager now, he flops down and swigs his coffee. Aaron raises a teasing eyebrow until Mosby nods over his shoulder. Through the door, hung in a tree, we see a trophy buck. Aaron roars, slaps Mosby's shoulder, and the coffee flies!

                    AARON (V.O.)
        Danged if he didn't believe me.
        Took to fightin' fearless, like a
        Alabama badger. After that, no mo'
        Jack. We took to callin' him John.

EXT. MOSBY FARMYARD - AFTERNOON

SUPER: FOUR YEARS LATER

A large home nestled in the lush Virginia countryside. A few slaves work in the surrounding fields.

INT. LIVING ROOM

MISS ABBY (30), her bun, spectacles, and Boston twang can't hide the beauty battling the blue-blooded old maid inside.

Mosby, now 17, but barely 100 pounds, his younger brother William, and their little sisters, Lucy and Lelia, listen with rapt attention.

                    MISS ABBY
        Just because slavery is in the Bible,
        does not mean God is commending it.
        He is only citing it as a fact of
        history, like a king or a war.

                    MOSBY
        But Miss Abby, we got slaves.

                    MISS ABBY
        You have slaves, John.

                    MOSBY
        Yes, Ma'am. We have slaves. So you
        think daddy's wrong having slaves?

                    MISS ABBY
        That is a question a great many people
        are asking these days.

                    MOSBY
        But does the Bible say it's evil?

                    MISS ABBY
        Is it right for a man to own another?
        To make someone do your work with no
        say or wage? See them as less than
        the thumb print of the Almighty,
        like so much as a horse or wagon?

                    MOSBY
        My pa says it doesn't call it sin.

The children all turn for her volley.

                    MISS ABBY
        My job here is to teach. Reading,
        writing, sums, <u>and</u> how to make up
        your own mind, John Mosby. To think.
        To be an adult. To be a real man.

They now all turn and look to Mosby. He stands up, puzzled, and moves to the window.

                    MOSBY
          My grandaddy, his grandaddy before
          him. Hard seeing them all wrong.

                    MISS ABBY
          So then, might makes right?

                    MOSBY
          No, but my pa says, Yankees telling
          us what to do with our own servants,
          ain't that the same, Miss Abby?

                    MISS ABBY
          Is that what Aaron and Absalom are?
          Servants? Stella serves in my home
          in Boston, whom I pay to do so. It
          allows me to tutor you, but she may
          leave if it suits her. She is <u>free</u>
          to choose.

Mosby looks out the window. Absalom, dressed in "hand-me-downs," too small for his teenage frame, works in the corral.

                    MOSBY
          My pa says if you treat them right-

                    MISS ABBY
          My pa says! My pa says! What do
          <u>you</u> think, John?

Absalom notices Mosby, smiles, and waves. Mosby acknowledges it, but half-hearted, almost ashamed.

                    MOSBY
          I reckon my pa knows what's best.
          They seem happy enough.

                    MISS ABBY
          Happy? I'll show you happy!

She stands, storms at him, and flings open the window!

                    MISS ABBY
          Yell out there, right now, and tell
          Absalom he's free! Go ahead! I
          dare you. Then you will see happy!

Mosby drops his head.

                    MISS ABBY
          John, I love you like my own son.
          It gives me no pleasure to quarrel,
          but you must stand up for what's
          right. That's what makes a man a
          real man. He takes a stand.

INT. LIVING ROOM - CONTINUOUS

The door to the parlor opens and the children's father, ALFRED MOSBY (50), enters with a heavy hush.

> ALFRED MOSBY
> Ready for the University of Virginia, John? With your permission, Miss Abby, time for John to become a man.

> MISS ABBY
> We were just speaking to that very point. Becoming a man, thinking for himself, and not what others think.

> ALFRED MOSBY
> More abolition talk? Thinking like yours will bring blood rivers to the South. Yankee tripe, telling us how to live. We will not be bullied!

> MISS ABBY
> Yet you tell Aaron how to live his life with the threat of a bullwhip?

> ALFRED MOSBY
> You have seen no whips here. We treat our servants well enough. Why without our help, they'd be lost. You think they have sense enough-

Aaron slips in unnoticed, and now uncomfortable.

> AARON
> 'Scuse me, Mister Alfred, sir. The wagon's all loaded, 'cept somebody crossed up the traces real bad.

> ALFRED MOSBY
> Yes, the new Clydesdales, full of piss and vinegar. Gave me some fuss.

> AARON
> No worry. I fixed 'em up proper. Mister John needing anythin' else?

> ALFRED MOSBY
> Thank you, no. That will be all Aaron. We will be out directly.

> AARON
> Yes, sir. I see to the buckboard.

Aaron backs out and Mosby begins to follow, but stops at the doorway to let his father pass first.

                    MISS ABBY
          Uh, Mister Mosby, you were saying?

                    ALFRED MOSBY
          Miss Abby, everyone here has slaves.
          Always has. Always will. It is
          legal. You can see Monticello from
          our orchard. Even Jefferson owned-

                    MISS ABBY
          And wrote "all men are created equal
          with the right to life, liberty, and
          the pursuit of happiness." Some
          would predispose upon our Creator in
          determining the who of "all men" is.

Alfred shakes his head and leaves. Mosby starts to go.

                    MISS ABBY
          John, please. Remember. A real man
          stands up for the weak. You of all
          people, should know that.

Mosby nods and follows after his father.

EXT. MOSBY FARMYARD - MOMENTS LATER

Mosby says his good-byes. Absalom, although nearby, is not
included. Alfred motions to his son to step away with him.

                    ALFRED MOSBY
          You are a man now, John. Miss Abby
          was right about that, but she could
          not be more wrong about our ways.
          You need to put her wagging tongue
          from your mind. Look at Absalom.

Mosby turns and sees his friend shoveling manure.

                    ALFRED MOSBY
          Animals. Without us, they are wild.
          Remember that. We have spared them
          from a cruel life, given them
          structure, protection, a family of
          sorts. In short, we have saved them.

Mosby can see Absalom over Alfred's shoulder. Absalom notices
him, but doesn't wave. Just a half nodded smile, and goes
back to work.

                    ALFRED MOSBY
          You hearing me clear, boy?

                    MOSBY
          I thought I was a man now, father.

                    ALFRED MOSBY
          You mind what I say, John. A real
          man knows his place. Blood comes
          first, then your country, Virginia.

                    MOSBY
          And friendship? Where does it rank?

                    ALFRED MOSBY
          Time you shed such childish notions.
          He is only a slave. Just property.

Mosby looks away, shakes his head, and laughs.

                    ALFRED MOSBY
          What, pray tell, is so amusing?

                    MOSBY
          Just seems all the folks who favor
          slavery...seem to all be free.

Aaron inches the buckboard toward them, but Mosby goes to
Absalom. Then, eyeing his father, Mosby hugs Absalom, hard.

                    AARON (V.O.)
          And that's the day I made up my mind
          'bout John Singleton Mosby.

EXT. DOWNTOWN CHARLOTTESVILLE - DAY

SUPER: UNIVERSITY OF VIRGINIA, CHARLOTTESVILLE

A circle of college boys near riot, surge around a rassling
match, cheering the ruckus on.

Mosby watches the two boys struggle in the greasy mud.

He notices George Turpin (20), across the circle, with some
disgust as Turpin swigs back a jug and rubs his mouth over
his sleeve, obviously too much Who-Hit-John.

Mosby turns back and roots for his friend, ARISTIDES (20),
who's clearly outmatched, and kicked into Mosby's arms.

As he does, a dark haired beauty on the crowd's edge, PAULINE
(20), catches Mosby's eye. He nods.

She smiles that Siren smile, and tilts her head.

                    MOSBY
          You look good!

                    ARISTIDES
          What fight you seeing? He's murdering
          me. Do me a favor, John? John!

                    MOSBY
          What? Sure, name it, Ari.

                    ARISTIDES
          Let him know I'm winning. My face
          would sure appreciate it.

                    MOSBY
          You'll be a Doc soon. Fix it later!

With that Mosby launches him back into the fray and sees a tipsy Turpin ogle Pauline, who then sneers at Aristides.

Turpin lunges, but misses Aristides, and sprawls at Mosby's feet. He grins at Pauline, then turns to redeem himself.

Mosby's foot intervenes and Turpin's face dozes mud as a constable forces his way into the fight, blowing his whistle.

Turpin swings his jug at Mosby, who ducks, and it crashes into the constable's head!

Turpin twirls and prepares another haymaker, but the crowd surges and Mosby collides with Pauline, pulling her down into his arms.

Turpin jabs at the air, and flies over a kneeling Mosby.

He recovers and rushes Mosby, who stands her up, and swings the constable's rifle.

Mosby misses Turpin, now absorbed in the counter swell, and nails a second constable. A THIRD CONSTABLE lifts Mosby up by the scruff of the neck.

                    THIRD CONSTABLE
          That'll do, sonny boy. You can cool
          your heels with us tonight.

Turpin, flopped in the mud-sloshed street, bids adieu through a liquored snarl, and slices his finger past his throat.

Mosby smitten, and unaware of Turpin's gloat, tracks Pauline's sweet smile, as does Turpin, whose face instantly darkens.

EXT. EASTER PARTY, CHARLOTTESVILLE TOWN SQUARE - EVENING

The town CELEBRATION. FIREWORKS, dancing, MUSIC, and food. Mosby inspects Aristides' black eye, until Turpin bursts in. About to come to blows, Pauline jerks Mosby onto the floor.

                    PAULINE
          A dance?

                    MOSBY
          Huh? Sure, in a minute. I was just-

                    PAULINE
          Now or never.

She leans in and whispers.

                    PAULINE
          I will not stand to have your skull
          cracked open by that drunkard Turpin.

                    MOSBY
          You're not giving me much credit.

                    PAULINE
          No real lady wants to be seen with a
          boy who's face is bandaged and
          swollen, John Singleton Mosby.

Mosby pulls back, but holds onto her hand.

                    MOSBY
          You know me?

She tugs him farther away. Turpin, reduced to a spectator, seethes. He lifts Aristides off the ground by his lapels.

                    GEORGE TURPIN
          You tell your pissant pal I'm gonna
          gobble him up. Raw!

He stomps into the darkness.

                    GEORGE TURPIN (O.S.)
          Noon, tomorrow! You tell that
          chickenshit twig I'm gonna' beat the
          tar outta' him!

As he exits, Mosby's mother, VIRGINIA MOSBY (51), approaches.

                    VIRGINIA MOSBY
          Aristides, who was that rude boy?

                    ARISTIDES
          I'm thinking trouble, Mrs Mosby.
          With a big, fat capital T.

EXT. BOARDING HOUSE - NOON

Mosby angles against the porch and scouts the street, both hands shoved into his coat pockets. Aristides whittles.

In the distance, a slew of boys round the corner.

                    MOSBY
          Bigger they are.

                    ARISTIDES
          About killed Sam Westin with a rock.
          You know that, right? Bled fierce.

Pauline strolls on the opposite sidewalk. She waves at Mosby,
but he doesn't notice, zeroed in on the gang behind her.

                    MOSBY
          About spent on the Turpin clan.
          Time one of 'em got some comeuppance.

She steps off the wooden sidewalk and waves again, then spots
what has Mosby's eye as the cluster passes her.

Turpin centers the mob, drops his head, and charges!

                    GEORGE TURPIN
          Arrrgghh! You're mine runt!

In an instant, the hulk bolts the stairs and swoops into
Mosby, who calmly pulls his hand out of his pocket and levels
a small pepperbox pistol.

Pauline clasps her mouth with both hands.

A muzzle flash drowns her shriek.

EXT. CHARLOTTESVILLE COURTHOUSE - MORNING

SUPER: TWO MONTHS LATER

Suited men dart up and down steps at a pillared courthouse.

INT. COURTROOM

Mosby sits with his lawyer. The prosecutor, WILLIAM ROBERTSON
(37), addresses the jury with extreme dignity and
sophistication. Mosby's family and Pauline fill the first
row. Slaves press against the windows outside.

                    WILLIAM ROBERTSON
          And so I commend this case of
          attempted murder to your wise
          discretion, a clear case of
          premeditation, imploring you, to
          award this hooligan his due justice
          for shooting a poor, unarmed boy.

The "boy" slumps opposite Mosby with his brother, NOBLE TURPIN
(35), and massages his bandaged throat. Noble's jagged black
beard crams his face making him seem older, darker, menacing.

JUDGE FIELD (63), turns to the jury.

> JUDGE FIELD
> Thank you, Mister Robertson.
> Eloquent, as usual. We are adjourned.

INT. COURTROOM - LATER

The jurors file in. All sit but the FOREMAN.

> JUDGE FIELD
> Have you reached a verdict?

> FOREMAN
> We have your honor. We find the
> defendant not guilty on the first
> charge of malicious shooting.

A big SIGH goes up.

> FOREMAN
> But on the second charge of unlawful
> shooting, guilty.

A GASP extinguishes it.

> FOREMAN
> We recommend the maximum sentence of
> one year in jail and a $500 fine.

Mosby's mother begins to weep as the frail teen shuffles away to jail. Noble Turpin grins, stands up, and applauds.

> GEORGE TURPIN
> (garbled)
> Year? Whadda' we do till then?

> NOBLE TURPIN
> Look over here.

They watch Pauline move to the window, where Aaron and Absalom crowd with other slaves, tearfully explaining the verdict.

> NOBLE TURPIN
> His heart ain't locked up.

EXT. CHARLOTTESVILE COUNTY JAIL - AFTERNOON

A man dozes in a chair on the porch. Citizens pass casually.

INT. JAIL CELL

A JANGLE of keys brings Mosby to his feet.

WILLIAM ROBERTSON
I was told you inquired after me.

MOSBY
Yes, sir. Wanted to thank you, sir.

WILLIAM ROBERTSON
Thank me? Indeed. How so?

MOSBY
I know talent when I see it, and you're all of that, sir. Always figured standing up required some size, but hang it, you opened up my eyes wide.

WILLIAM ROBERTSON
Did I now?

MOSBY
Yes, sir. When Judge Field gave you the nod, I figured the Law has made a good deal out of me, so I thought I would make something out of it. I mean, if you'll teach me.

WILLIAM ROBERTSON
Teach you? I don't believe-

MOSBY
Hardly believe it myself, 'cept my own eyes took it all in. Just words. Who'd a figured? You were a sight to see, sir. Real poetry in motion.

WILLIAM ROBERTSON
You do realize I am responsible for your present incarceration?

MOSBY
I do, and that's why I chose you. My mind's made up. Figure I got a year to study up on it. That is, if I can get a look-see at your books.

WILLIAM ROBERTSON
Let me be clear. You wish to become an attorney?

MOSBY
I sure do. Yes, sir.

WILLIAM ROBERTSON
In jail, and fancy me as your tutor?

                    MOSBY
          And as a friend too, I hope. I'm
          not what you made me out to be, which
          makes it all the more impressive.

Mosby extends his hand through the bars. Robertson studies
it for a moment, and then clasps it.

                    WILLIAM ROBERTSON
          Very well, I accept your proposal,
          if only to see what other wonders
          lurk behind those demon blue eyes.

EXT. CHARLOTTESVILLE TIMES OFFICE - NIGHT

George Turpin and a MEAN-FACED MAN (38), sidle up to the
newspaper office, assess the street, and slink inside.

INT. TURPIN'S OFFICE

Noble Turpin sets the print type on the press. The door
jingles open and slams.

                    GEORGE TURPIN
             (raspy whisper)
          S'all set. Lotsa' talk 'bout the
          Governor's pardon though.

                    MEAN-FACED MAN
          I still say we wait.

                    NOBLE TURPIN
          No. Tonight, Justice takes a peek.

He removes a pepperbox pistol from his desk, the same one
Mosby dropped at the boardinghouse, and puts it in his belt.

EXT. SCHOOL YARD - NIGHT

A rope creaks and twists under the weight below the branch
of the schoolhouse oak. Hooded men ride away, but one stays.

                    KLANSMAN
          I'll be needing this. You won't.

A hand raises something to the flour-sacked face to inspect.
Moonlight glimmers off a nail ring.

                    KLANSMAN
          Retribution, Mosby. Tombstone cold.

He rides off into the night, the same direction as the others,
and we see the dangling man is black.

INT. JAIL CELL - NIGHT

Mosby cries and hugs Aaron through the bars, who wails pitifully. Alfred stands nearby with Virginia and Pauline.

                AARON
    My sweet, sweet Abby! Who'd go and
    do my precious baby boy dis' way,
    sweet Jesus?

                MOSBY
    So help me, we'll find him. I promise
    on my soul, Aaron.

He removes his nail ring and gives it to Aaron.

                MOSBY
    You have my solemn word.

INT. JAIL CELL - AFTERNOON

Mosby slides his lunch tray under the bars, uneaten.

                PAULINE
    Not partial to my cooking? That
    could be a problem in our future.

                MOSBY
    Locked up, killer loose. Even Aaron's
    future looks brighter than ours.

                PAULINE
    You gave him that ring. Why?

                MOSBY
    He made them, for Absalom and me.
    Just kid stuff. Then it was, anyway.

                PAULINE
    The way he put it on, seemed more
    like a diamond ring to him. Think
    he'd make me one?

                MOSBY
    I think he knows the only ring you'll
    have on your finger will be from me.

She blushes and, through the bars, he takes her hand.

INT. JAIL CELL - AFTERNOON

Mosby sits at a book strewn table. William Robertson stands nearby, reading. Mosby slams the heavy law book closed!

                    MOSBY
          Something about Abby's ring.

Robertson removes his spectacles and waits.

                    MOSBY
          If Turpin, settling up for George,
          why send it to me? It's too obvious.

                    WILLIAM ROBERTSON
          What year is it?

                    MOSBY
          1859.

                    WILLIAM ROBERTSON
          Lawyering now for going on 15 years,
          John. Logic dictates one of two
          things. Either he did not do it and
          someone wants you to think he did.

                    MOSBY
          Or?

                    WILLIAM ROBERTSON
          Or Turpin did it and doesn't care if
          you know it or not.

                    MOSBY
          Meaning what?

                    WILLIAM ROBERTSON
          Meaning you're next. And with the
          Governor's pardon, you are a target
          that moves now. I suggest you do
          just that. Pauline's from Bristol.
          Maybe it's a good time to go and
          meet her folks.

EXT. NASHVILLE HOTEL - AFTERNOON

SUPER: NASHVILLE, TENNESSEE, 1860

The burnt brick hotel, anchored in snow, towers over a muddy
street with but a few riders bent against the snowy wind.

INT. BALLROOM

Mosby and Pauline's wedding RECEPTION. Her father, BEVERLY
CLARKE (50), approaches with SENATOR ANDREW JOHNSON (50).

                    BEVERLY CLARKE
          Pauline, allow me to introduce Senator
          Andrew Johnson. Senator, my daughter
          Pauline and her husband, John Mosby.

ANDREW JOHNSON
Congratulations! A pleasure, dear.

PAULINE
We are deeply honored, Senator.

MOSBY
Please stay, enjoy some refreshments.

ANDREW JOHNSON
My regrets. I fear I must return to Washington posthaste. South Carolina has created quite a stir.

BEVERLY CLARKE
As a sovereign state, surely she is-

ANDREW JOHNSON
A traitor! To the Union and a reproach to the true South we all hold dear. We will beat her into submission, sir. Trounce her soundly, by whatever means necessary!

BEVERLY CLARKE
And Virginia? If she follows her?

ANDREW JOHNSON
These are strange days, Beverly, but I promise any rebel state who follows her will receive no quarter from me. Mississippi, Florida, Alabama. All buzzing with secession rants. Idiots!

BEVERLY CLARKE
Buzzing indeed. Kicked over the beehive. Lincoln's election, I mean.

MOSBY
So father tells us, time after time.

ANDREW JOHNSON
Indeed. Time is of the essence. With your permission, Ma'am. Sir.

The Mosby's nod. Johnson and Beverly take their leave.

Mosby's parents step up, hugs and handshakes all around.

ALFRED MOSBY
John. Pauline. We know how fond you are of this and so, well, we want you to have it. Congratulations!

Alfred hands Pauline an ornate envelope. Pauline opens the gilded envelope and shows Mosby the document.

                      MOSBY
     Why, father. I do not-

                  VIRGINIA MOSBY
     Our pleasure.
         (to Pauline)
     They are excellent in the kitchen.

                  ALFRED MOSBY
     And superb with horses, eh, John?

                    PAULINE
     I'm speechless. I don't-

                  VIRGINIA MOSBY
     I know you've taken quite a shine to
     him, Pauline. Now don't do anything
     foolish, like setting him free.

Awkward laughs.

                  ALFRED MOSBY
     Poor old buck would not know what to
     do with himself anyway. Never quite
     the same after Absalom. Remember,
     John. They are like a good dog.
     Train them, care for them, but
     remember, always wild. He's outside.

Through the window, in the buckboard, flurries layer Aaron's slumped shoulders and a shivering bundle of belongings.

                    MOSBY
     What about his family?

                  VIRGINIA MOSBY
     Oh, he can see them when you visit.
     Now enjoy your day! Best see to our
     guests, Alfred. Excuse us, dear.

Alfred and Virginia part, waving down old friends.

Pauline steps to the window and taps the glass. Aaron looks up, returns her wave, and forces a smile.

                    PAULINE
     Promise me, John. We do all we can
     for his happiness. For Absalom's
     sake we make him happy. Always.

Mosby holds her, kisses her cheek, and nods.

EXT. THE U.S. CAPITOL, EAST PORTICO - AFTERNOON

SUPER: LINCOLN'S INAUGURATION, MARCH 4, 1861

The half completed Capitol Dome behind him, LINCOLN (52), stands before 30,000 and adjusts his steel-rimmed spectacles. A black tower, solemn and slender, he matches the day's gloom.

> LINCOLN
> In your hands, my dissatisfied fellow-countrymen, and not in mine, is the momentous issue of civil war. The Government will not assail you. You can have no conflict without being yourselves the aggressors. You have no oath registered in Heaven to destroy the Government, while I shall have the most solemn one to "preserve, protect, and defend it."

He pauses and squints as the sun breaks through the clouds. Looking up, with a faint smile at the omen, he continues.

> LINCOLN
> I am loath to close. We are not enemies, but friends. We must not be enemies. Though passion may have strained it must not break our bonds of affection. The mystic chords of memory, stretching from every battlefield and patriot grave to every living heart and hearthstone all over this broad land, will yet swell the chorus of the Union, when again touched, as surely they will be, by the better angels of our nature.

EXT. MOSBY FARMYARD - MORNING

Miss Abby, in the buckboard with Robertson, wipes her eyes. Bags of luggage jam the back with Aaron.

> MOSBY
> I am sorry. Father gets so excited.

> MISS ABBY
> Secession will mean war and force everyone to take a stand. Mine is at home, with my family, where I can help those who have no voice.

> PAULINE
> Yes, you should be with family.

MOSBY
We understand, Miss Abby.

MISS ABBY
Do you, John? Who will stand up for the unfree? For Aaron? Even Absalom, God rest his soul, demands a voice.

Aaron pretends not to listen and secures her trunk and satchels, but Absalom's name moves him.

MISS ABBY
The middle is no place for a man. The Lord spits out the lukewarm.

WILLIAM ROBERTSON
She's right, John. This country is like an old pair of trousers with a new patch. It cannot stay together long. Something has to give.

MOSBY
South Carolina is bluffing. It's just politics. Virginia will not leave the Union.

MISS ABBY
And if she does, what will you do?

MOSBY
I'm no Secesh. All I want is to be left alone, help folks with their law needs, and raise a family.

WILLIAM ROBERTSON
John Brown was not bluffing. The rope on his neck was a fuse and Charleston is blowing on it. Fort Sumter is a powder keg, John.

MOSBY
I cannot see it coming to much.

WILLIAM ROBERTSON
Well, I hope so. We best be going. Trains north are antsy these days, won't wait long for us nasty Rebels.

MOSBY
Come home safe, Will. Plenty of hotheads on the roads these days, what with Turpin's rabble stirring the pot. Be careful. Miss Abby.

She leans down and hugs him for a long time.

                         AARON
               Don't you worry none, Master John.
               I take good care both these children.

EXT. CAMDEN STATION, BALTIMORE - LATE AFTERNOON

While Robertson says good-bye to Abby, Aaron stays with the
buckboard. One line of cars faces north, with a door ajar.
Several black hands fumble to close it.

                         RUNAWAY
                    (whispered loud)
               Hey Buck! Yo', Buck!

Aaron turns, sees the hands, glances down the track at
Robertson, then moves to help.

                         RUNAWAY
               Come on, Buck. Hop in. We goin'
               ride the freedom train!

His hand raised to the door, Aaron begins to pull it open,
sees Absalom's nail ring, and stops.

                         RUNAWAY
               Whatchoo' waitin' on? Come on!

                         AARON
               Afraid's not my time just yet. Lord's
               luck to ya'll though.

He slams it. The iron shackle clanks shut.

EXT. COUNTRY ROAD - EVENING

Aaron and Robertson head south in the gathering dusk.

                         WILLIAM ROBERTSON
               Thought about hopping that train?

                         AARON
               Notion did tumble past my mind.

                         WILLIAM ROBERTSON
               I would not have thwarted you.

                         AARON
               Yes, sir. Figgered it that way.

                         WILLIAM ROBERTSON
               You could be free this very moment.

                    AARON
          Well sir, I reckon I already is,
          insides anyway. Got some choices
          yet, and a promise I means to keep.

                    WILLIAM ROBERTSON
          What is that, in the road? Appears
          to be a man. Pull over, Aaron.

EXT. BUCKBOARD - MOMENTS LATER

The Mean-faced Man sags between Aaron and Robertson.

                    WILLIAM ROBERTSON
          You need a doctor.

                    MEAN-FACED MAN
          I said I'm fine. Just winged some.

                    WILLIAM ROBERTSON
          You could lose your leg. That bullet
          should come out. Could be trouble.

                    AARON
          Trouble already here mebbe. Yonder.

They approach a Federal checkpoint. Two Yankee soldiers
step clear of the group and wave them to stop. As the rig
slows, shots RING out and the two sentries topple over.

The Mean-faced Man drops his smoking pistol, snatches the
reins, and lashes the team through the rush of Yankee militia,
flipping Robertson backward into the wagon.

CRACK-ZING! CRACK-ZING! CRACK-ZING!

Robertson recovers, stands back up, and grabs at the reins.

CRACK-ZING! CRACK-THUMP!

Then lurches forward, onto Aaron, a bullet hole in his coat.

CRACK-ZIP! CRACK-ZIP! CRACK-ZIP! CRACK-WUMP!

The Mean-faced Man's head flops to the side, brains ooze.
Aaron seizes the reins, and shoves him out of the buckboard.

FA-LUMP!

                    AARON
          Yah! Yah! Git on up, there! Yah!

Robertson, blank, rolls onto the floorboard, and coughs blood.

                        AARON
            Oh, Lord. Help us fly, sweet Jesus!

EXT. DOWNTOWN CHARLOTTESVILLE - AFTERNOON

SUPER: CHARLOTTESVILLE, VIRGINIA, APRIL, 17, 1861

Aristides tears across the street to Mosby's law office.

INT. MOSBY'S OFFICE

Mosby at his desk, an engraved Bowie knife prominently displayed before him.

"Stand up for those without a voice." -Will Robertson

A RUCKUS outside. Aristides shoots in, excited.

                        ARISTIDES
            John! Best come quick! Looks bad.

EXT. STREET

They race to the shot up buckboard, by the telegraph office.

Aaron cries in the front seat, head in his hands, blood and brains on his shoulder. A crowd in back pulls out the body.

                        MOSBY
            Let me through! What happened?

Aaron leans down.

                        AARON
            It was Yankees, Mister John.

                        MOSBY
            How? Why?

                        AARON
            We give this fella' a ride, next
            thing, everybody shootin'. Bad luck
            is all. Jonah luck. Mister William,
            he git shot. Man they wanted git
            shot, so I shoved 'im and lit out.

Mosby has Robertson cradled in his arms, weeping.

                        AARON
            It was horrible. Jes' horrible.

                        MOSBY
            Miss Abby?

                    AARON
          We tooks her to the train awright,
          but comin' back...it was turrible.

Noble Turpin blasts out of the telegraph office, brandishing
a telegram!

                    NOBLE TURPIN
          To arms! Virginia secedes! To arms!

PANDEMONIUM! SHOUTS and GUNFIRE bombard the mourners.

The jubilant throng engulfs the wagon and smothers Mosby's
anguished bawl. He crushes the body to his, and convulses.

EXT. MOSBY'S HOME - DAWN

An ashy fog swirls the outline of a quaint farmhouse, and
reveals Aaron, mounted, holding the reins of three other
horses. Beyond him, ghostly figures tramp the misty road.

INT. KITCHEN

Mosby's uniform sags off his bony shoulders. Pauline slides
foodstuffs into a haversack with great care, and swabs tears.

They embrace, as ranks of men march past their home, guns
bob in a leaden stream flowing north. DRUMS and FIFES spar.

Mosby pulls away and heads out to join them, stops, and comes
back to hug Pauline one last time.

                    MOSBY
          I have to go, you know that. All my
          life I have wanted to do battle when
          great things were at stake, when it
          really mattered, when everything
          hung in the balance. This is it, my
          moment, my destiny. You understand.

                    PAULINE
          You're sure...about Aaron?

                    MOSBY
          He taught me to fight. He
          understands, believe me.

                    PAULINE
          But we promised. His happiness,
          always. Just doesn't seem right.

MOSBY
Pauline, we are invaded. I am
fighting for you, for our babies not
yet born, for Virginia, our country,
not its politics. Try to see it
that way.

PAULINE
But Virginia's freedom means his
bondage. Does it really mean more—

MOSBY
Virginia is my mother's name, same
as our great state, and I'd gladly
die for both. But know this my dear,
I intend to live, and to fight, as
never before, because this time it
is for everything we are and own.

They hug and he mounts, drifting into the gray flood rushing by, but Aaron tarries.

AARON
Don't you fret none, Miss Pauline.
I tooks a vow. Lord and me, we got
an understanding now, 'bout Mister
John. We seein' to him, personal.

She removes her shawl and hands it up to Aaron.

PAULINE
Thank you, Aaron. They'll be some
cold nights. To remember home.

She takes his hand, sees the nail ring, and squeezes.

PAULINE
I want you both back, hear? You're
family now. Like Absalom. Family.

Too overcome, he nods, and trots after Mosby.

EXT. REBEL PARADE GROUND - DAY

In varying shades of gray and butternut, 100 men in scraggly lines that hardly resemble an army, confront rows of canvas tents with swords, flintlocks, and antiquated shotguns. Slaves and boys hold their mounts in the rear.

BIG YANKEE AMES (22), a tree trunk of a man aptly named, in Union britches, arrives late and crashes through the line of horses, bowling Aaron over.

He tosses his reins to a boy, and hurries to join the ranks. Everyone notices, but only Mosby steps out of line and approaches him. Mosby motions Ames to bend down, whispers, pats him on the shoulder, and returns to formation.

Ames goes back to Aaron, dusts off his shoulders, mumbles a few words, shakes his hand, and hurries back to his place.

He leans forward to look down the row at Mosby, who nods.

EXT. REBEL PARADE GROUND

A bugle BLOWS and four officers step out of the center tent.

GRUMBLE JONES (41), shabbier than some recruits and a stark contrast to the young officers behind him, bearded and bald, grimaces like something is too tight.

Mosby, in the front row, recognizes one of the officers as Noble Turpin! WILLIAM CHAPMAN (24), steps past Turpin.

                    MOSBY
  Son of a-

               WILLIAM CHAPMAN
  Ehhhh-Tennnn-Hut!

The men straighten, but unsure what's been decreed exactly, and shuffle into a slightly better line.

Turpin moves to the front and throws out his chest.

                NOBLE TURPIN
  Gentleman! I am Lieutenant Noble
  Turpin. Many of you here know me.

He recognizes Mosby and smirks like a lamb with two mammies.

                NOBLE TURPIN
  Let me welcome you to the Washington
  Mounted Rifles and to thank you for
  coming to the aid of Virginia. To
  lead our sacrifice for state's rights,
  I present Captain William Edmondson
  Jones. As your grandfathers fought
  for Virginia with General Washington-

                GRUMBLE JONES
  Awright, awright. That'll do, Turpin.
  Ain't fawkin' running for office.

Grumble strides to the line, scratches his crotch, and launches a tobacco juice stream near the closest man.

                    GRUMBLE JONES
          You sumsabitches think this is a
          damn camping trip. Impress the girls,
          steal some kisses, wave the flags.

He walks past the first row, dresses them down with his eyes.
Each man recoils as he passes, as if a skunk let loose.

                    GRUMBLE JONES
          A glory picnic, is it? Kill some
          Yanks and home in a week. Well, I
          hate anyone pissin' down my back, so
          here it is, ramrod straight. Most
          of you poor bastards ain't coming
          back from this here La-tee-dah. JEB
          Stuart, another damn dandy thinks
          he's a soldier cuz he sticks feathers
          in his fawkin' hat, says I'm to make
          soldiers outa' you sow's ears!

He strolls ever closer as he moves.

                    GRUMBLE JONES
          Shitfire! Might's well ask me ta'
          pull rabbits out a my ass, but there
          it is. I'm crazy enough ta' take
          the job, and salute his feathered
          chicken shit costume too. Damn
          peacock!

Brown juice splatters off a recruit's bare foot. The officers
follow at a respectful distance.

                    GRUMBLE JONES
          Those who think they know me don't
          like me. Complain too much. Cuss
          too much. Smell like shit. Grumble.

Jones looks sideways for any sign of a snicker.

                    GRUMBLE JONES
          Ain't no fawkin' Quaker meeting now,
          ladies. You are here to kill fawkin'
          Yankee bastards 'for they kill you.

He stops to look at Ames, leans in, sniffs, and scowls.

                    GRUMBLE JONES
          Nice drawers, big Yank. Lose 'em,
          and the hair tonic. Smell like a
          Nawlins strumpet.

                    BIG YANKEE AMES
          Yes, sir. Right away, sir.

Jones continues to saunter past the men.

                    GRUMBLE JONES
    Number one. All men die, so git
    over it. Two. Don't worry what I
    think of you. I don't give a rat's
    ass about anybody, especially
    officers. Just do your job. Three.
    If you run, my bullet, your back.

He walks down the next row.

                    GRUMBLE JONES
    And four. Experience is a good
    teacher; only a fool won't learn.
    Remember that and maybe you'll live
    to bitch to your grandkids about
    Grumble Jones. I may not save your
    saddle sore ass, but I'm gonna kick
    it into soldier shape. If not, well,
    the hell with you, and your damn
    passel a' grandkids. You can all
    kiss my brown spot!

Some CHUCKLE, including Mosby, until Jones stops behind him and comes back to the first row.

                    GRUMBLE JONES
    Funny am I, shit-for-brains? Kind
    of a wee prick for fawkin' with such
    a big Yank. Dead in a week. Well?

Mosby doesn't flinch and stares past Jones.

                    MOSBY
    Never paid much mind to size, sir.
    All the same. Big Yanks, big mouths.

More SNIGGLES. Jones steels his eyes on Mosby and drills in, nose to nose.

                    GRUMBLE JONES
    That sassy ass squint says it all.
    Come to whip-ass Yankees, eh? Fawkin'
    tough little shit, are we now? Your
    momma must be worried sick, runt.

He grins and steps back.

                    GRUMBLE JONES
    What'd ya' say ta' the Big Yank?
    Darkie something special is he now?

                    MOSBY
    Consider him kin, and told him so.

                    GRUMBLE JONES
          Kin? Shit for brains sure. And?

                    MOSBY
          Suggested he get it right, or he'd
          be crapping lead by lunch.

                    GRUMBLE JONES
          Hah! Big splash from a little pisser.
          Figure ta' whip him in a fair fight?

                    MOSBY
          Fair ain't much of a strategy, sir.
          A good mount and a dry Colt seems to
          even most of the Lord's oversights.

Jones smirks. He likes his spunk.

                    GRUMBLE JONES
          Gotta' name?

                    MOSBY
          Mosby, sir. John Singleton Mosby.

                    GRUMBLE JONES
          Where you hail from?

                    MOSBY
          Outside Charlottesville.

                    GRUMBLE JONES
          Glory be! We're neighbors. What do
          you do now?

                    NOBLE TURPIN
          He's a lawyer, sir.

                    GRUMBLE JONES
          A shyster! And a scrawny one ta'
          boot. You two friends, are ya' now?

                    NOBLE TURPIN
          He shot my brother, sir. Unarmed.
          Spent seven months in jail.

                    GRUMBLE JONES
          Do tell!

                    MOSBY
          A bully and a drunk, learned him
          about fighting...fair, sir.

Grumble looks impressed and leans in to study Mosby's eyes.

                    GRUMBLE JONES
          Window to the soul, some say.

He looks him over again, as if for the first time.

                    GRUMBLE JONES
          I ain't got a soul, but I make a
          fine Bristol stew. Come ta' my tent
          tonight. We'll fatten you up. A
          good wind and I'll lose you. Turpin!

                    NOBLE TURPIN
          Sir!

                    GRUMBLE JONES
          Add a plate ta' my mess.

                    NOBLE TURPIN
          But sir, Mosby is a Union sympathizer-

                    GRUMBLE JONES
          Hell, we're all fawkin' Americans,
          for God's sake! Worst part of this
          disaster. Went ta' fawkin' West
          Point with Buford, for the love of
          Mike!

Turpin scowls as they pass, and Mosby lips a kiss.

                    NOBLE TURPIN
          This ain't over, nigga' lover.

                    MOSBY
          What I love ain't your concern.
          What I hate concerns you plenty.

EXT. GRUMBLE'S TENT - EVENING

Two silhouettes on a tent wall. Grumble, LOUD, STAMPS around
inside, arms flail. Mosby seated, nods, and writes furiously.

                    AARON (V.O.)
          Took a shine to the Colonel right
          off, learned him up on soldiering,
          like he was his own. Come to find
          he got the bitters on a'counts his
          wife and boy, got ripped out his
          arms in a shipwreck, rest their souls.

                    GRUMBLE JONES (O.S.)
          Napoleon? Tactics dead as his big
          toe. Cavalry attacks, fast and close.
          Defend it, you're dead. Mobility!
          Audacity, always audacity. Can't
          hit what ya' can't catch. Aim for
          the shined buttons. Without brass,
          an army dies. And no damn sabers.
          Revolvers up close, more the better.

                    MOSBY (O.S.)
          So get rid of my sword?

                    GRUMBLE JONES (O.S.)
          Hell no! Fawkin' great for roasting
          meat over a fire!

Outside, the LAUGHTER slams hard against a brooding Turpin.

                    AARON (V.O.)
          That snake didn't cotton to all
          Grumble's fuss, poisoned up the men.
          Made it 'is business to upend the
          Colonel every chance he got, but 'ol
          Mosby never did sit pat on a hand.

EXT. REBEL CAMP - DUSK

Mosby stands by the fire. Behind him, two dozen troopers
wash up at the Shenandoah. Shadows fall off the campfires,
but you can still see movement against the dimming sky.

                    BIG YANKEE AMES
          Stuck like a cork in a jug!

                    MOSBY
          Plenty of fresh water for the horses.

                    WILLIAM CHAPMAN
          A blind mule can see this is a trap.
          Jones would ream you good, backing
          up to this river, war games or not.

                    MOSBY
          Aaron, you partial to this site?

                    AARON
          Makes cookin' and cleanin' up easy
          for this old Virginny boy, yes sir.

                    BIG YANKEE AMES
          And half our men out looking for
          Turpin. You're asking for it, Mosby.
          At least put out some videttes to
          give us a warning. Something.

              WILLIAM CHAPMAN
          Or a sign, "Come get the greenhorns."

Mosby sips his coffee and scans the sunset horizon. With
the firelight's glare, no one notices the shadows shift in
the trees around them.

                    MOSBY
          Maybe you're right about vid-

                    RIDER
          Hands up! So's we can see 'em, Mosby!

                    BIG YANKEE AMES
          Damn it!

                    MOSBY
          Looks like we're too late, boys.

                    RIDER
          Get your men out of their tents!

Within seconds, Turpin's 80 men trot out from the trees and
surround the camp. Turpin saunters in last, beaming.

                    NOBLE TURPIN
          Game over. Back against a river?
          Tsk, tsk, tsk. Gonna' be mighty
          painful for Grumble, bringing his
          pet back home as my prisoner. What'd
          he say? Experience is a good teacher.

Mosby forms a pistol with both hands, squints and slowly
aims it at Turpin's head, and then continues pointing over
his head until it's almost straight up into the trees.

Turpin and his men lift their eyes to see...

50 pairs of Colt muzzles pointed down at them, along with
showers of cascading laughter.

                    MOSBY
          And only a fool won't learn.

EXT. REBEL CAMP - EVENING

Mosby writes on his knee, while Aaron cooks over the campfire.

                    MOSBY (V.O.)

"My Dearest Pauline,

I take pen in hand now to write you a few lines and to wish you a most happy birthday. I hope it is our only one apart. I am getting along first rate. Aaron cares for my every need like a doting mother hen.

I have not prayed about it, as you suggested, but even if I did, where would he go? Surely not North-"

                    AARON
          Pining for home, Mistuh John?

Aaron offers Mosby a coffee cup on a plate of beans.

                    MOSBY
          Pauline's birthday.

                    AARON
         Do tell? Never did know my day.

Mosby puts down his letter and turns up his face.

                    MOSBY
          Never had a birthday?

                    AARON
         Oh, slave gettin' born ain't no call
          for fussin'. Recollect the night
          Abby come 'round though. Christmas
          eve it was. Baby Jesus never smiled
          as sweet as my Abby done that night.

Mosby sets his plate down and sighs.

                    MOSBY
          Get the blues if I think on him too
          much. Puts one in mind of home.

                    AARON
         Never figgered he beat me to the
          grave no-how, but leastways he free.

                    MOSBY
          Yes, I suppose he is that.

Both men just take that in for a silent minute.

                    MOSBY
          If you were free, would you go North?

                    AARON
         Oh, reckon not, not without the wife.
          Her heart busted up bad on Abby dying.
          Kith and kin first, my daddy always
          said. Couldn't just up and leave-

The night vomits Noble Turpin into their lap, while his
teenage slave holds at the edge on his haunches.

> NOBLE TURPIN
> I hear right? Got a boy dead? Pity.
> Some want all you colored dead, but
> not me. Miss out on all this fun
> killing Yankees, not for you colored.

Noble leans down into Aaron's face.

> NOBLE TURPIN
> Die badly, did he?

> MOSBY
> This poor man lost-

> NOBLE TURPIN
> Man? What kind of Southerner are
> you, Mosby? He's an animal, like
> all them. A damn dog. Go! Sit!

Aaron backs up toward Mosby and sits next to him on a log.

> MOSBY
> You're over the line, Turpin.

> NOBLE TURPIN
> You would take up with 'em, you Yank
> lover. Animal's all they is.

Turpin motions his slave into the light.

> NOBLE TURPIN
> Git on in here now, Rastus!

He relishes the power.

> NOBLE TURPIN
> Can yours do tricks? Lick'em, boy!

His slave flops down and SLURPS his muddy boots. Mosby turns
away, but Aaron watches in wonder.

> NOBLE TURPIN
> This is what you're fighting for
> Mosby, to keep our way of life, the
> way we see fit to live it. So our
> pets can do parlor tricks. Enough!

The slave scurries off to the dark edge and cowers.

                    NOBLE TURPIN
          Never forget it. Got my eye on you,
          and your damn lackey. Grumble ain't
          everywhere, all the time.

Turpin stomps off, his slave loping alongside.

Both men just stare at the coals.

                    MOSBY
          Damn it!

He flings his coffee into the fire.

                    MOSBY
          I hear you thinking. Go on, say it.

                    AARON
          Think mebbe you shot the wrong Turpin.

Mosby glares at the flames.

                    MOSBY
          Gonna be a long damn war.

                    AARON
          Well sir, mebbe this war take care
          his kind, one way or other. Good
          Lord, He steers them bullets straight.

EXT. BATTLEFIELD, VIRGINIA - DAY

SUPER: BATTLE OF MANASSAS, VIRGINIA, JULY 21, 1861

Bull Run. A smoky July sun winces at 60,000 butchers.

Mosby leads a cavalry scout into the woods. Mangled bodies, two and three deep, welcome him with each SLOOSHING step.

An artillery volley CRACKS the sky, thankfully drowning the wounded MOANS of dying men all around them in its THUNDER.

                    MOSBY
          Drive these woods! Clear their
          pickets and pressure those guns.

                    ARISTIDES
          Not seeing much fight way over here.

                    MOSBY
          Just scouts today, Ari. Plenty of
          hot work yet. First, their artillery.

They salute and Aristides leads them toward the deadly SNAPS.

Mosby dismounts and crawls up a rise, avoiding the twisted dead. He peers over a bloated horse and eight Yankee troopers spot him.

MOSBY
Thunder!

Turpin and Grumble, both glassing the battle, see Mosby run back down the hill, but to their surprise, he grabs two revolvers from two dead soldiers nearby and turns around!

GRUMBLE JONES
I'll be fawkin' damned ta' perdition's flames. That Mosby's got spirit. No brains, but plenty a fight!

NOBLE TURPIN
He's a dead man.

GRUMBLE JONES
We need more men like that. Get over there and help him, Turpin.

NOBLE TURPIN
More like bring back his body.

Turpin turns his mount and heads toward Mosby.

Three of the Union troopers are shot from their saddles. The rest continue. Mosby kneels and shoots two more. A third thinks better of it, and turns back downhill.

The two remaining cavalrymen hesitate and Mosby empties his other Colt, hitting both. They turn and give it up.

Turpin arrives behind Mosby and levels his pistol at him.

NOBLE TURPIN
Tombstone cold.

Mosby spins. Turpin's revolver misfires. Mosby pulls Robertson's Bowie knife, hesitates, and then lowers it.

MOSBY
Don't mistake mercy for kindness. We will finish this, but now's not-

BAH-WHOOM!

An artillery round CRASHES into both men who recoil into the dirt strewn air. Turpin evaporates in the shower of debris.

When Mosby comes to, Aristides swabs his forehead, and sloshes a canteen into his mouth.

EXT. FIELD HOSPITAL - EVENING

A large brick mill bustles, wounded men hive at every entrance, and approaching wagons CREAK under the dead weight.

Another wagon, stacked with arms and legs, sits beneath a second story window. From the bottom, blood drips into a black pool. From above, a steady thump of limbs drop into the mound of tattered flesh and jutting bones.

Two UNION OFFICERS light cigars over a lantern nearby.

Anguished CRIES for mother and ghoulish HOWLS stab the air.

Mutilated corpses litter the farmyard, blue and gray, laid out like sticks of wood in some garish child's game.

Below another window, piles of severed limbs kick or claw at the air in frozen moments of horror.

> UNION OFFICER 1
> I tell ya' it is true. Heard it from old man McDowell myself. Lost an arm at Sumter and they figured him a Reb. Some hospital mix up.

> UNION OFFICER 2
> Quibley? A spy? Dumb as a post.

> UNION OFFICER 1
> Just sayin'. Jeff Davis' office.

> UNION OFFICER 2
> You snortin' Elmer's Pop Skull again?

> UNION OFFICER 1
> Go ta' blazes. Tell ya' I heard it.

Both men slog off into the darkness as a corpse rolls out from under a mangled jumble of bodies. Unrecognizable, he drags himself toward the doorway with one arm and collapses.

Two ORDERLIES see him flail in the entrance, place him on a litter, and take him inside. He gurgles one word.

> ORDERLY 1
> What's he saying? Quietly?

> ORDERLY 2
> Quickly, I think. He's an officer. Best fetch him right up to the Doc.

> ORDERLY 1
> Easy Reb. Your war's just a memory.

                    NOBLE TURPIN
          M'naimshs eesh'turpin.

EXT. GRUMBLE'S CAMP - DAY

Mosby huddles with the other officers behind Jones, seated in front of his tent, presiding over a map cluttered table.

                    AARON (V.O.)
          Weren't long 'fore Grumble made the
          Colonel his Adj-a-tant.

Mosby leans in, fingers a route on the map, and Grumble nods.

                    MOSBY
          A deer run, parallels Balls Ford, if
          we walk the horses, can't be seen.

                    GRUMBLE JONES
          Where do they hook up? Next map.

Grumble signals for more maps, as a dashing rider pulls up.

                    DISPATCH RIDER
          Captain Jones?

                    GRUMBLE JONES
          Who wants ta' know?

                    DISPATCH RIDER
          General Stuart sends his compliments,
          sir. I am to wait for your reply.

He hands a dispatch to Mosby, who hands it to Grumble.

                    GRUMBLE JONES
          Does he now? Whippersnapper still
          wearing a silly costume like yours?
          Crack-brained, high-falutin'....

The rider looks confused.

                    DISPATCH RIDER
          Sir?

                    GRUMBLE JONES
          Ah, wasted on the young.

He opens it, scanning, annoyed.

                    GRUMBLE JONES
          Fawk my greasy legged gram-mammy!
          Wants us ta' escort some floozies
          ta' his fawkin' dance! Do I look
          like a fawkin' chaperone for that
          feathered fop?

He shoves the paper back to Mosby.

                    GRUMBLE JONES
          You tell that damn dandy that Hell-

                    MOSBY
          Sir, I know these women, well one of
          them. Acquaintances of my wife.

                    GRUMBLE JONES
          Do tell.

                    MOSBY
          Yes, sir.

                    GRUMBLE JONES
          Then the fawkin' job is yours, Mosby.
          Tell Jimmy James Ewell Brown we are
          happy ta' oblige. My Adjutant will
          see ta' it.

                    DISPATCH RIDER
          With your permission, sir.

EXT. GRIGSBY HOUSE, STUART'S HQ - NIGHT

Mosby steers the carriage into the farmyard with a woman on either side, all three thick with snow.

INT. LIVING ROOM

JEB STUART (28), swings in, his flair and panache fills the room, striking Mosby with instant awe. He snaps to attention.

                    JEB STUART
          At ease. You're wet to the hide.
          Come, dry yourself by the fire.
          Miss Emily and Miss Doreena?

                    MOSBY
          Thank you, General Stuart. Lieutenant
          Mosby. Your Lieutenant Colonel
          Blackwood is seeing to their needs.

                    JEB STUART
          War and dancing, both need partners,
          eh, Mosby? Give me that wet coat.

                    JOSEPH JOHNSTON (O.S.)
               JEB, are you coming or not?

                    JEB STUART
               In a minute, General. Let me see to
               our soggy friend first. It's late,
               stay the night and dry out.

                    MOSBY
               Thank you, no. I just need a horse-

                    JEB STUART
               Nonsense. Come and meet General
               Johnston and General Smith. A fat
               rooster has made the ultimate
               sacrifice for state rights.

                    MOSBY
               General Johnston? *The* General
               Johnston? And G.W. Smith?

Stuart leaves as Mosby moves toward the fire.

                    JEB STUART (O.S.)
               Mosby! Generals do not wait long.

                    JOSEPH JOHNSTON (O.S.)
               Except for artillery!

They all LAUGH. Mosby scratches his head.

                    MOSBY
               Generals Johnston *and* Smith? Jiminy!

Mosby leaves the fire and edges toward the dining room.

INT. DINNER - LATER

GENERAL JOSEPH JOHNSTON (56), pulls Mosby into their banter.
Old, but their best general in every way, he seeps dignity
and respect. Every Confederate general defers to him.

                    JOSEPH JOHNSTON
               Sir, you cannot be serious. They'd
               rise up, another Turner revolt.

                    MOSBY
               They are Virginians first, sir.

JEB and GENERAL SMITH (42), both choke, and brace for
Johnston's counter charge.

                    JEB STUART
               That'd starch a few drawers, sure!

                    JOSEPH JOHNSTON
          Why that's political suicide, if
          Davis even discussed it in Richmond.

                    MOSBY
          You said conscription wasn't working.
          We're out-manned near three to one.

                    GENERAL SMITH
          Arming slaves? Preposterous! That
          dog won't hunt.

                    MOSBY
          Pardon me, sir, but mine would fight
          for me. Wouldn't yours do the same?

                    GENERAL SMITH
          You think your boy would fight, of
          his own free will, if he had one,
          when he receives nothing in return?

                    MOSBY
          They'd fight for home, same as us.
          And if they fight, maybe-

                    JEB STUART
          Maybe what?

                    MOSBY
          Maybe, in exchange, we offer them
          their freedom.

A canister shot at 10 yards couldn't have silenced men
quicker. The generals just look at each other as Mosby
continues eating, undaunted. JEB smirks.

                    MOSBY
          This rooster is quite good!

                    JOSEPH JOHNSTON
          Yes, a very surprising bird indeed.

EXT. GRIGSBY HOUSE, STUART'S HQ - MORNING

Mosby saddles JEB's horse, saying his good-byes to Emily and
Doreena. Stuart and Johnston step out onto the porch.

                    JEB STUART
          Remember, Grumble rubs you raw.

                    GENERAL JOE JOHNSTON
          Or JEB's singing gets on your nerves.

Both men laugh and Stuart points at Mosby.

                    JEB STUART
          Always shade under my tree for a
          good scout, ya' hear?

Mosby mounts up and turns his new horse to go.

                    MOSBY
          Sir, it would be an honor, but my
          loyalty is to Captain Jones. I will
          see your horse is returned.

Mosby salutes, but JEB just tips his hat. General Smith
joins them on the porch.

                    JEB STUART
          Nervous ya' some to be up front,
          colored toting loaded guns behind?

                    GENERAL SMITH
          Down Texas way, his sorta' talk gets
          a boy strung up as not.

EXT. GRUMBLE'S CAMP - AFTERNOON

A cavalry squad pounds hard into Grumble's camp. Jones and
a smattering of officers just watch, unimpressed.

FITZHUGH LEE (29), in the lead, pulls up in a dust bath.
Wide and stern, he seems put out just having to breathe.

                    FITZHUGH LEE
          Captain Jones?

                    GRUMBLE JONES
          Depends. Who wants ta' know?

                    FITZHUGH LEE
          Colonel Fitzhugh Lee. A word with
          you, sir. In your tent.

                    GRUMBLE JONES
          Bobby Lee's nephew? Thought you was
          a captain.

                    FITZHUGH LEE
          A colonel now, and my family is not
          germane to our affair. If you please.

Fitz rides to the tent. His men start to unpack his gear.

                    GRUMBLE JONES
          Germane? I smell fawkin' Richmond.

EXT. GRUMBLE'S TENT - MORNING

Mosby dismounts, hands his reins to Aaron, and enters.

INT. GRUMBLE'S TENT

His salute stalls when he sees, seated before him, Fitzhugh!

              MOSBY
     Lieutenant Mosby, sir.

            FITZHUGH LEE
     I expect my adjutant on post.

             MOSBY
     Yes, sir. Captain Jones had sent-

            FITZHUGH LEE
     Jones is no longer of any consequence.
     You will be of like value if you're
     not available when I need you, son.

He continues signing documents, never looking up.

            FITZHUGH LEE
     Reviewing this report from Turpin.
     Pity. Hard to find good officers.

Now he looks up, biting a mouthful of bees.

            FITZHUGH LEE
     Warnings in here about you. Sense
     of entitlement. Suck up to Jones.
     Reluctant Unionist. Abolitionist?

            MOSBY
     Sir, Turpin held a grudge-

Fitz drops his head and returns to his papers.

            FITZHUGH LEE
     Bad form to mock the dead, Lieutenant.
     Need a man I can rely on, implicitly.

Mosby does not answer or move. Finally, Fitz looks up.

            FITZHUGH LEE
     Your politics worry me down, son.

            MOSBY
     Sir, if my abilities or honor seem
     deficient perhaps-

            FITZHUGH LEE
     Both are in the balance right now.

                    MOSBY
          Perhaps my resignation-

                    FITZHUGH LEE
          Resignation accepted. You are
          dismissed, Private Mosby.

EXT. GRIGSBY HOUSE, STUART'S HQ - LATER

Stuart sits on the porch and looks up from a report when
Mosby reins up with JEB's horse.

                    JEB STUART
          Hello there, Mosby! Change of heart?

                    MOSBY
          Kinda' got decided for me. Company
          voted Grumble out.

                    JEB STUART
          Ah, yes. Fitz. Saw that order.

                    MOSBY
          Got the impression he did not prefer
          my services, so I was hoping-

                    JEB STUART
          Then you are free to join my staff!

                    MOSBY
          Immediately, it would appear, General.

                    JEB STUART
          JEB. Call me JEB.

He thumps the report against his hand and points it at Mosby.

                    JEB STUART
          How would you feel about probing
          McClellan's right cheek? Jackson
          could use a little gander, know what
          he's up against.

                    MOSBY
          Stonewall? Yes sir! I'll need some
          men, and a fresh horse.

                    JEB STUART
          Already assembled. Keep my horse.

                    MOSBY
          Then, in a few days, Gen...uh, JEB.

                    JEB STUART
          Believe in divine appointments, Mosby?
          I do, and I think the good Lord sent
          you to me, for some grand purpose.

                    MOSBY
          Well, I hear He steers bullets, but
          steering me might not come so easy.

EXT. STUART'S CAMP, NEAR RICHMOND - MORNING

SUPER: THREE DAYS LATER

Hooves thunder the dust up as Mosby and his men arrive at
Stuart's new camp. He dismisses them and rides toward a
shady tree where Stuart dozes on the ground.

Mosby stretches out beside his commander and tickles JEB's
nose with his ostrich plumed hat.

                    JEB STUART
          Mosby!   What news?

                    MOSBY
          His right flank, hanging out like
          Old Abe's drawers on wash day.

                    JEB STUART
          You're joshin'!

                    MOSBY
          Rode all the way around his army.

                    JEB STUART
          In his rear? Impossible!

                    MOSBY
          Cocky scoundrel has not even
          considered our cavalry might want to
          visit, maybe borrow some wagons.

                    JEB STUART
          Divine, indeed! I need this in
          writing. I'm off to Lee. Can you
          have it in 30 minutes?

Mosby cocks his hat and winks a "need you ask."

EXT. DOWNTOWN WASHINGTON - AFTERNOON

The Capitol Dome, still under construction, rises over a
muddy street filled with construction wagons, horses, and
vast coils of troops. Wounded men clump everywhere.

INT. UNION HOSPITAL

Three DOCTORS stand around a heavily bandaged patient.

                    FIRST DOCTOR
          Should be dead. Lost a lot of mass.

                    SECOND DOCTOR
          And blood. Does he even know yet?

                    TURPIN
          Know what?

The OLDER DOCTOR, steps closer and sits down.

                    OLDER DOCTOR
          That you are going to be exchanged.

                    TURPIN
          And the good news?

                    OLDER DOCTOR
          I'm glad you have a humor. You'll
          most likely be needing it.

                    TURPIN
          Give it to me straight out.

                    OLDER DOCTOR
          Very well. Just below the knee, we
          had to take it all off. Your arm
          may heal, in time. Your face has....

Turpin's curdled face absorbs the ugly news and turns away.

                    OLDER DOCTOR
          Gangrene, settled in your orbital-

                    TURPIN
          Any others, from my unit?

                    SECOND DOCTOR
          You were our only Rebel off-

                    TURPIN
          Was a Mosby brought in? Small man?

                    FIRST DOCTOR
          No. Just you. A friend?

                    TURPIN
          Not so's you'd notice.

EXT. LEE'S HQ - NIGHT

A stone farmhouse sits above the road, moon smattered tents below, fires snap, horses seem to sway to a SQUEAKY fiddle.

INT. KITCHEN

WALTER TAYLOR (26), Lee's adjutant, peeks around the door. His voice, thin, cool, and exacting, seen as much as heard, resonates like Lancelot with Arthurian reverence.

                    WALTER TAYLOR
          Pardon, sir. General Stuart.

LEE (56), an aristocratic blend of old Virginian grace and West Point granite, stands, tugs his vest, and puts on his tunic. Serious, but quiet eyes command immediate respect as the South's only true Monarch. A marble man to both sides.

                    LEE
          Splendid. Splendid. Send him in.

                    JEB STUART
          General Lee, sir.

                    LEE
          Welcome! A success I trust?

                    JEB STUART
          Sir, over 100 wagons, 166 prisoners,
          260 horses and mules, and bushels of
          small arms. Compliments of McClellan!

                    LEE
          Wonderful news, General Stuart.
          Wonderful. Your casualties?

                    JEB STUART
          Two men. One dead, one captured.

                    LEE
          Your scouts are to be commended.

                    JEB STUART
          Yes, sir. Tried out a new man, a
          remarkable fellow. John Mosby.

                    LEE
          Mosby? The name is new to me.

                    JEB STUART
          That will surely change, sir. Led
          us around McClellan's whole army!

                         LEE
               Fully around? Another Lincoln tongue
               lashing for Little Mac, to be sure.

                         JEB STUART
               I'm sure his scapegoat is in place.

Both men laugh and move to the sitting room.

                         JEB STUART
               Mosby did propose a new idea. Harass
               the Union rear with mounted
               guerrillas. Hit trains, telegraph,
               supply lines. In the spirit of
               Francis Marion.

                         LEE
               Washington's Swamp Fox. My father
               served with him in our first
               Revolution. That would tie up troops
               meant for our front. It has merit.

                         JEB STUART
               He has the necessary skills. Whip
               smart and flat out fearless.

                         LEE
               Give him a few men, see if he can
               make an impression. Now tell me
               more about your ride around McClellan.

                         AARON (V.O.)
               Gen'rl Lee seen right off what the
               Colonel seen. Put a fox with no
               fear in the henhouse, no tellin' who
               gets riled worse, hens or the farmer.

EXT. CONFEDERATE WHITE HOUSE - MORNING

SUPER: RICHMOND, VIRGINIA, 1862

A deliberate Turpin canes each step up a long stairway and
finally enters the White House.

INT. JUDAH BENJAMIN'S OFFICE

An eye patch and a partial mask hide most of what was Turpin's
face. The cane steadies his peg leg as the CLERK (24),
reviews his papers.

                         CLERK
               Let's see. Manassas. Believed dead?

                    NOBLE TURPIN
          Wounded. Secretary of State Benjamin,
          if you please. It's urgent.

                    CLERK
          Always is. I'm sorry, but the
          Secretary is in conference all morn-

He turns and we see his sleeve is pinned up.

                    NOBLE TURPIN
          Lose that arm at Sumter?

                    CLERK
          Why yes. How did you-

                    NOBLE TURPIN
          Quibley isn't it?

                    CLERK
          Have we met, sir?

Turpin points with his cane toward the door behind the clerk.

                    NOBLE TURPIN
          Ah, Mister Secretary-

Quibley turns as Turpin's cane, in full swing, lifts him out
of his chair with a skull and cartilage crushing roundhouse!

EXT. CONFEDERATE WHITE HOUSE, COURTYARD - AFTERNOON

Ten Confederates shoulder rifles and FIRE. A one-armed man
jolts off his coffin, legs scissor the air, and then falter.

INT. JUDAH BENJAMIN'S OFFICE

The bearded and round-faced JUDAH BENJAMIN (53), presides
from an open window. Turpin studies the mark on his cane.

                    JUDAH BENJAMIN
          Philippe what, may I ask?

                    NOBLE TURPIN
          Mal de Fezint, from New Orleans.

                    JUDAH BENJAMIN
          We are in your debt, Mister Mal de
          Fezint. We seem to have an opening,
          perhaps we could return the favor.

                    NOBLE TURPIN
          Please, Philippe. And it would be
          my honor, sir.

EXT. VIRGINIA COUNTRYSIDE - DAY

SAM CHAPMAN (23), brother to William, and a handsome ministry student, rides with Mosby and Aristides to face a dozen rough "men" on horses who look like they've never even held a razor.

                    ARISTIDES
     Form up, boys.

                    SAM CHAPMAN
     Boys, indeed.

                    MOSBY
     Younger the better. No fear of dying.

Sam smartens the line, while Mosby drums his saddle horn.

                    MOSBY
     I am John Singleton Mosby.

Expecting more man in the saddle, the teens mumble.

                    MOSBY
     You may know my officers. Dr.
     Aristides Monteiro and Sam Chapman.

They trot forward, nod, and reverse their horses smartly.

                    MOSBY
     Riding with me is earned, a
     privilege, one easily lost to a spot
     in the infantry. Only the best stay.

More whispers.

                    MOSBY
     Our grandfathers beat the British
     because they fought my style of
     warfare. I have but two orders:
     Mount up and follow me. Obey that
     and you can stay, once you learn how
     to fight proper. For now, we train.

                    AARON (V.O.)
     What the Colonel had here was a whole
     mess a' baby Alabama badgers, and
     not one gave a hang 'bout no Beast.

MONTAGE - TRAINING THE 43RD TO FIGHT

-- Mounted men race past, reins clenched in their teeth, and empty both pistols, one after another, as the targets erupt.

                    MOSBY (V.O.)
          We will not fight fair. Always
          attacking. Lightning raids. Take
          it to them, gentlemen, use their own
          fears to cripple any resistance.

-- The horsemanship is superb. Men hang on the sides, shoot
over their saddles, under their horse's neck and belly, and
sport double-neck holsters to magnify their firepower.

                    MOSBY (V.O.)
          We will not use the saber. The Colt
          revolver, up close, is our weapon of
          choice. That, and sheer audacity.

-- Two men fly down the road, a gang of Rangers in pursuit,
until riders pour out on either side, an ambush rehearsal.
Rounds splat targeted trees, nearly all center kill shots.

                    MOSBY (V.O.)
          You keep the spoils. Horses, money,
          guns, food. Keep it all or burn it.

-- Union troopers, hands in the air while Rangers inspect
pistols and horses, get steered off the road into the night.

                    MOSBY (V.O.)
          Four pistols and two horses each,
          compliments of our Yankee visitors.

-- A train rams into a ditch and accordions in upon itself.

-- Telegraph poles, greased in flame, twist and topple over.

-- Wagons torched, as Yankee prisoner columns ride south.

                    MOSBY (V.O.)
          We'll live with civilians and share
          our bounty with them in thanks.

-- Safe houses. Trap doors, false walls, and floorboards
hide the men, while Union soldiers search in vain.

                    MOSBY (V.O.)
          Without a camp, we cannot be found.
          We will divide, hit them in concert,
          and seem larger. Soldiers love their
          sleep, so we'll take that too. A
          tired trooper is easily scared, making
          poor decisions. Our ally will be
          the night, as well as the good folks
          in the valley.

-- A boy's silhouette swings a hilltop lantern, a light
answers from a distant barn, and another winks on the horizon.

                    MOSBY (V.O.)
          When I need you, I will signal you.
          Until then, we train. Tell your
          friends. If they have no family,
          can ride, and shoot, I want them.
          The younger the better.

EXT. VIRGINIA COUNTRYSIDE - CONTINUOUS

Mosby turns his horse to leave, but Aristides stops him.

                    ARISTIDES
          What about uniforms, John?

                    SAM CHAPMAN
          Yes, what should they wear?

Mosby surveys his new Rangers, and smirks.

                    MOSBY
          Something gray. Just tell them to
          wear something gray.

MONTAGE - RAIDS ON UNION TROOPS

-- Federal wagon trains flame and crackle as Rangers escort
prisoners and horses into the woods. Each Ranger carries
some booty-pistols, carbines, and foodstuffs.

-- Yankee couriers, hands up, pouches lifted by sword tip.

-- A train careens into an embankment, thudding metal clangs
and screeches, showers of sparks spew, the boiler blows!

-- Horses get shooed from a corral, while four Union
sentinels, gagged and tied, roll around on the ground.

-- Yankees ransack homes and root through barns, empty-handed.

EXT. VIRGINIA WOODS - NIGHT

A penetrating rain soaks two shadows who emerge as slickered
riders. Mosby nods to Big Yank, who lifts his arm and 28
riders slide out of the forested darkness.

                    BIG YANKEE AMES
          Right there, that dip. Splits both
          Yankee videttes. Natural blind spot.

                    MOSBY
          I know.

                    BIG YANKEE AMES
          You know?

                    MOSBY
          Scouted them three days ago. You
          passed your first test, Big Yank.

EXT. FAIRFAX COURTHOUSE, VIRGINIA - CONTINUOUS

The riders, and two gagged Union sentinels, snake into town.
A Ranger shinnies up the pole and clips the telegraph wires.

                    MOSBY
          No shots, horses and officers only.
          Take the telegraph officer out first.
          You two, where's General Stoughton?

The sentinels exchange looks, shrug, and nod at the home
behind Mosby.

                    MOSBY
          Obliged. Sam, Ari, Yank, with me.

The Rangers rap hard on the door until the window flies open
above the porch. LIEUTENANT PRENTISS (27), leans out.

                    LIEUTENANT PRENTISS
          Aw right, dammit, aw right. A minute.
          What's so damn important?

                    MOSBY
          Captain Miller, Fifth New York, an
          urgent dispatch for the General.

                    LIEUTENANT PRENTISS
          On a night like this, what the Hell!

The door opens. Mosby's muzzle jams into Prentiss' cheek as
he's forced back inside.

INT. VESTIBULE

                    MOSBY
          Welcome to Virginia. I'm John Mosby.

                    LIEUTENANT PRENTISS
          Never heard of you.

                    MOSBY
          You will after tonight. Stoughton?

They drift upstairs to GENERAL STOUGHTON's (26), room. Empty
bottles and dainties litter the floor, betraying his recent
playboy antics. Mosby pulls back the sheets and smacks his
bare butt!

                    GENERAL STOUGHTON
          What the blazes! Do you know who I
          am, Mister?

                    MOSBY
          Do you know Mosby, General?

                    GENERAL STOUGHTON
          Yes, do you have the rascal?

                    MOSBY
          No, but he has you!

                    AARON (V.O.)
          General up and quit the war after he
          got exchanged. His name got all
          used up in the papers, but that splash
          made some big ripples, especially in
          the Colonel's own mind. Some he
          hadn't even thunk up...yet.

EXT. CONFEDERATE SECRET SERVICE HQ - DAY

A red brick building next to the Confederate White House.

INT. TURPIN'S OFFICE

Mael de Fezints throws a newspaper down. The headline reads: *"Mosby Shames Federals, General Stoughton Kidnapped!"*

EXT. WHITE HOUSE - MORNING

Behind a statue of Jefferson, one soldier leans on his musket at the front door, as people come and go without fanfare.

INT. LINCOLN'S OFFICE

Lincoln studies reports. EDWIN STANTON (50), contrasts Lincoln in every way, bespectacled, bearded, round, short, and tense. He steps up with more papers and telegrams.

                    EDWIN STANTON
          Right under our noses! A general,
          33 prisoners, and 58 horses! Imagine!
          What will the country say?

Lincoln reads, unruffled, accustomed to Stanton's outbursts.

                    EDWIN STANTON
          Well? They'll blame us, you know!

                    LINCOLN
          Oh, not too jimmied 'bout a general.
          I can make one with a pen stroke,
          but 58 horses. Mighty hard to replace
          them at $125 a piece.

EXT. COUNTRY ROAD - NIGHT

A line of supply wagons pop and burn, dead Yanks in the road.

EXT. YANKEE CAMP - NIGHT

Camp tents collapsed, flapping in flames. Troopers, frozen
in grotesque and unnatural death twists are strewn about,
some smoldering over the fires, unconcerned, bubbling.

EXT. RAILROAD - NIGHT

An engineer pulls his train brake, and looks back at a mess
of telegraph poles jumbled and snapped in his wake, yanked
free by his passing cars.

EXT. MOSBY'S CAMP - EVENING

A small encampment of Rangers rise at the thump of hooves.

AUDIE (19), hops down with the ease and grace of a pine
squirrel. LEWIS POWELL (21), oozing strength and defiance,
like one big muscle with a head, stays mounted. WAT BOWIE
(24), grabs the bridle of Powell's horse.

                    WAT BOWIE
          Whadda' we got here, Audie?

                    AUDIE
          Says he wants to join the cavalry.

                    WAT BOWIE
          Who doesn't? Where you from, Tiny?

                    LEWIS POWELL
          Second Florida. Got nicked up some
          at Gettysburg. Heard about you fellas
          in the hospital, down in Washington.

                    MOSBY
          Whaddya' go by there, Florida?

                    LEWIS POWELL
          Lewis Powell, but most call me Doc.

                    MOSBY
          Had supper, Doc?

                    LEWIS POWELL
          Ain't eaten since day before.

                    MOSBY
          Well, Aaron'll get you some vittles.
          Get some rest. We got big doings in
          the morning. We'll give you a try.

Mosby walks off. Powell dismounts as Aaron walks up.

                    LEWIS POWELL
          You got negroes riding with you?

                    WAT BOWIE
          Aaron cooks, goes with the Colonel.
          He knows his place.

Aaron hands him a knife and fork with the plate.

                    LEWIS POWELL
          Allowing them knives too?

Aaron turns to leave and Powell digs in.

                    LEWIS POWELL
          Dang, this is mighty fine grub! Hey
          Buck, get me some more these beans.

Aaron doesn't stop walking.

                    AARON
          That's alls we gots left.

Back at the chuck wagon, Aaron strokes the mules, then dumps
the beans out at their feet, almost a full pot!

EXT. MOSBY'S CAMP - EVENING

Mosby pockets a letter and stabs at the dying flickers, while
Aaron cleans up the pots. Mosby sighs long and hard.

                    AARON
          Miss Pauline?

Mosby nods.

                    AARON
          Lucky to have such a fine woman.
          Best part a bein' away. Makes you
          'preciate something when you ain't
          got it no more.

                    MOSBY
          Never been apart before this. Easier
          for the men without any family.

                    AARON
          Yes sir, ain't never had a thing,
          then, less misery going without as
          not, I 'spect. Less missing to it.

                    MOSBY
          Right now, I'm missing sleep. Wake
          me in two hours. Looks like rain.

Mosby rolls over and pulls a gum blanket up around his legs.
Aaron looks like he wants to say more, but shakes it off.

                    AARON
          Well sir, mebbe a visit, when we
          gets closer to the Miskel place.
          Hathaway's ain't far off, if Miss
          Pauline could gets through the lines.

Mosby sits up, and gives him a hard look.

                    MOSBY
          You brought somebody to mind just
          now. Always looked out for me too.

                    AARON
          Do tell. Fella' I know?

                    MOSBY
          Yeah, you raised him.

EXT. MISKEL FARM - EARLY MORNING

Powell steps from the farmhouse, stretches, strolls the porch, and admires the sunrise, then freezes. Something's not right.

Birds burst skyward. Trees glint? Scabbards CLINK! HOOVES!

He breaks for the barn!

EXT. BARN

Wat opens the barn door, toe to toe with a breathless Powell!

                    LEWIS POWELL
          Yanks! Get up! Move! Move!

Men barrel past, a blur of saddles, boots, and revolvers!

The only escape, a high-fenced entry, surges with blue riders.

Mosby leads 30 men from the corral into 150 Yankees, pistols crack lethal puffs as saber wielding troopers drop, falter, and recoil.

Lead stunned, the Yankees hesitate, bunch up, then a mob retreat, crushed together as 40 more Rangers join the rout.

A murderous fire empties Union saddles, the fallen trampled grunt and scream. Now a rout, those Yanks not shot, break and ride back to the main road. All but a few are cut down.

EXT. MISKEL FARM - EVENING

Wounded and dead Union soldiers litter the lane. Two DOCTORS, heads shaking as they move among the carnage, spy a wounded officer, CAPTAIN BEAN (30), who struggles in vain to stand.

> TALL DOCTOR
> Easy there, Captain. Lie still.

> CAPTAIN BEAN
> Had them penned in, and they charged!

> SHORT DOCTOR
> What's your name, Captain?

> CAPTAIN BEAN
> Last thing I expected. Outnumbered, surprised, cornered. Damnedest thing.

> TALL DOCTOR
> Rest easy there, son.

> CAPTAIN BEAN
> A kid led it. Just a little shit, fought like the dickens though. A holy terror. Maybe 16, 17 tops.

> SHORT DOCTOR
> According to that wounded Reb over there, that "kid" was Mosby.

EXT. MOSBY'S CAMP - NIGHT

Small fires light up faces, chatting, smoking, and laughing.

> MOSBY (V.O.)

My dearest Pauline,

I take pen in hand to tell you I am well, and well fed. The Yankee sutler wagons provide more than enough for Aaron to impress at the cook fire, even preparing General Sheridan's oysters last night.

Several Union wagons, crashed into one another, burn in a massive pyre that roars into the night sky, illuminating dead Federal troopers all over the road.

MOSBY (V.O.)

He is a good deal thought of now, his hoe cakes something the men hanker for and devour with great relish. It is curious to see him so resolute in his duties, knowing our victories may cost him dearly, an unspoken tale between us.

Aaron moves amongst the Rangers, slopping out dinner. Most of the men warmly thank him, Wat and Powell not so much.

MOSBY (V.O.)

I try not to think too deeply on this, and perhaps your prayers are at work, but it does wear when I see his loyal friendship so tested by our success in battle. Yet he does not complain or even wince at our celebrations.

Aaron hands Mosby a coffee cup and he lowers his letter.

MOSBY
Ah, smells like home.

AARON
Powder 'bout all I smellin' today.

MOSBY
The Gray fought well this morning.

AARON
Been puzzlin' on that very thing.
Ever wonder how comes we wearin'
that particular color?

MOSBY
Gray? Never gave it much thought.

AARON
Well sir, I sho' have. Seems right
fittin' too when ya' study on it.

MOSBY
Please, enlighten me, mighty Phoebus.

AARON
Seems to me, this here war all 'bout
rights. And one of them rights is
havin' a say on sending me where
white men figger I needs to be.

MOSBY
And that's gray?

                    AARON
          From my side da crick? Yes sir, it
          sure do seem something gray's cloudin'
          up that water. Fighting for rights
          and liberty with one hand.

Aaron hands him a plate of ham hocks and cornbread, and then
switches hands and pulls it away.

                    AARON
          But holding it back with the other.

Aaron offers it again and Mosby takes his plate.

                    MOSBY
          Deep down, you know I had no choice
          in this fight. Our country, our
          families. Our very-

                    AARON
          Freedom, I knows. It's your family's
          ground, you and Miss Pauline's home.

                    MOSBY
          It's your home too, as much as ours.

                    AARON
          That's the grayest part. Freedom, I
          mean, exactly what is it?

                    MOSBY
          Do what you want, when you want.

                    AARON
          Well sir, mebbe it is, mebbe it ain't.

                    MOSBY
          These shoulders been handling your
          truth for years, Aaron. Don't start
          riddling me now. Just spit it out.

                    AARON
          Seems to me, the way of it is this.
          Freedom's bigger than homes and wants,
          but still simple enough to sort out,
          easy as falling off a log.

He sits down on the log, next to Mosby, man to man.

                    AARON
          Means you do right when it needs
          doin', no matter what folks say, you
          do it cuz you gots the strength,
          here, inside, to <u>choose</u> to do right.

MOSBY
'Cept sometimes doing the right thing
can end mighty wrong, get folks hurt.

AARON
Like when you hugged my Abby?

Mosby drops his eyes, studies his plate a while.

MOSBY
Yeah, that hurt Pa, but needed doing.

AARON
Oh, falling off stings, sure. Ain't
sugaring it up none. But stepping
off, on purpose, like you done?
Harder to do on 'counts you need one
mo' thing.

MOSBY
What's that?

AARON
Well sir, once you off the log, you
still gots to stand up. And standing
up, well, that takes a real man to
stop something he knows ain't right,
'specially when he sees how sharp it
might stick him.

MOSBY
Sounds more like courage.

Aaron stands up and looks down on Mosby.

AARON
Yes, sir. Two peas, same pod.

EXT. RAILROAD - NIGHT

Shovels pry a train track rail free. It's wrapped in
telegraph wire, replaced, then strung out to nearby bushes.

EXT. THE WRECK

The wire tightens and jerks the rail free.

A train engine tilts, a massive crash and explosion, cinders
fly, SCREAMS, and YELLS scorch the air. The engine flames
as the crumpled cars fold up on it like a pocket knife.

Rangers hurl down the bluff, women and children yanked from
the wreckage. Above, Mosby directs his men, who rob everyone.

                    SAM CHAPMAN
          Bunch a Dutch, Colonel. Won't budge.

                    MOSBY
          Then burn the Germans out.

Blazing newspaper bundles sail into the doorways and windows,
followed by the tumbling Germans, who get quickly fleeced.
Sam roots through some luggage, stands, then waves at Mosby.

                    SAM CHAPMAN
          Gonna' want a gander here, Colonel.

Mosby comes down and looks into two canvas duffel bags.

                    MOSBY
          Thunder! Somebody in blue ain't
          getting paid this month.

                    SAM CHAPMAN
          Must be $200,000 in greenbacks!

                    MOSBY
          Divvy it up at Aldie's. Equal shares.

The two PAYMASTERS watch Sam leave, then protest.

                    OLD PAYMASTER
          Federal train, destroyed and robbed.
          They'll hang you for this, Mosby.

                    MOSBY
          Me? They oughta' hang Sheridan.

                    YOUNG PAYMASTER
          General Sheridan? Why?

                    MOSBY
          Isn't it his job to protect all this?

EXT. COUNTRY ROAD - NIGHT

Mosby rides with one of the prisoners, an old PRUSSIAN MAJOR
(60), in a fine beaver coat and hat, very posh and haughty.

                    MOSBY
          Why come over here to fight us, Major?
          We've done nothing to you.

                    PRUSSIAN MAJOR
          Ve come learn American var tactics,
          Yankee artillery, cavalry, lessons
          you maybe now learn the hard vay
          yourself at Gettysburg, ya?

He chuckles and rides ahead of Mosby.

EXT. COUNTRY ROAD - DAWN

DOLLY RICHARDS (22), rail lean and all business, races up to Mosby at the head of the column.

                    DOLLY RICHARDS
          Problem with the Dutch major, Colonel.

Before an irritated Mosby can answer, the major barges in.

                    PRUSSIAN MAJOR
          I protest, damn them to Hell. Your
          men take my clothes, give these rags!

Dolly fights a smirk, and hides it behind his hand.

                    MOSBY
          You came to learn our tactics, right?

                    PRUSSIAN MAJOR
          Ya, so vhat?

                    MOSBY
          Well Major, here's your first lesson.

EXT. VIRGINIA COUNTRYSIDE - NIGHT

SUPER: HATHAWAY HOUSE, MIDDLEBURG, VIRGINIA

A brick Greek Revival styled mansion, immaculate, and nuzzled against a colossal black walnut tree, faces the misty Blue Ridge Mountains.

INT. MASTER BEDROOM

The Mosbys in bed, stare at one another. A full moon shines through an open window, scattering the massive branch shadows all over them in a crazy mottled pattern.

                    PAULINE MOSBY
          John, tell me the truth, is it over?

                    JOHN MOSBY
          Sooner than Richmond wants, I suspect.

                    PAULINE MOSBY
          So many families. I hear things,
          John. Bad things. Horrible stories.

JOHN MOSBY
Oh, we're minding the store here alright, I guess. Ruffled Custer and Sheridan's feathers plenty. Still ain't gobbled me up yet.

PAULINE MOSBY
But the army? General Lee. Are they...are they spent?

JOHN MOSBY
Visited Petersburg. 'Bout broke my heart, Pauline. They're starvin'. Boys are eating, well, it's not good, that's all. Trenches everywhere. Every night, men just up and quit.

PAULINE MOSBY
How long can General Lee last?

JOHN MOSBY
Grant's nipping at his heels, digging closer every day. A month. With some luck, maybe June. I dunno.

She snuggles deeper into him and closes her eyes.

PAULINE MOSBY
Seems like a bad dream that we'll never wake up from.

JOHN MOSBY
Unless something changes, something real big, waking up may be the worst part for General Lee.

INT. LINCOLN'S OFFICE - MORNING

Lincoln licks his thumb, and flips through some telegrams. The same staff brace for his reaction. GENERAL MESSNER (56), waddles up to Stanton.

GENERAL MESSNER
No camp or pattern, just burnt wagons, derailed trains, wires cut, horses stolen, dead troopers. And more friends than a graveyard has ghosts.

EDWIN STANTON
And Sheridan's payroll, $173,000! They know every inch of that valley. He appears, then, like a ghost, poof!

                    LINCOLN
          Do not confuse audacity with spirits,
          Mister Stanton. He's mortal, like
          all of us. Let's not make him into
          some kind of a gray ghost, shall we?

EXT. TRAIN STATION - AFTERNOON

Steam and smoke swirl around a locomotive that gushes and
slows. On the rear car platform, GRANT (42), smokes a stub
and chats with CUSTER (25).

Grant's beard, short, thin, and unremarkable mirrors the
man. Custer's tailored uniform, golden locks, and blood red
scarf make Grant's plain private's tunic all the more stark.
When you're the top dog, you don't need to put on the dog.

In the distance a dust cloud swells and catches Grant's eye.

                    GRANT
          Them boys ours, Custer?

                    CUSTER
          No flags, General. Must be Rebs.

Below, the STATION MASTER (67), clears his throat.

                    STATION MASTER
          If'n he seen your train 'fore them
          troopers, you'd a had a warm
          reception, sure.

                    GRANT
          You know those men?

                    STATION MASTER
          Sure, and your boys'll be havin' a
          hot howdy doo here right quick.
          These parts, everybody knows him.

                    GRANT
          Him?

                    STATION MASTER
          Gray Ghost.

                    GRANT
          Mosby! I should like to meet him.

                    CUSTER
          With a good stout rope.

                    STATION MASTER
          Thunderbolts shootin' out my toes at
          Christmas more likely than stringing
          him up, Sonny.

                    CUSTER
          We could wire ahead, General. The
          5th New York could nab him easy.

                    STATION MASTER
          'Fraid the wires are down, thanks to
          'ol Mose, but ya'll are welcome to
          wait. He'll be here directly.

                    GRANT
          How do you know that?

                    STATION MASTER
          Put on a fresh pot. He can smell
          coffee a mile off. Stay and see.

                    GRANT
          Reckon not. We're due in Washington.
          Best chalk it up to Providence.
          Just the same, thanks.

                    STATION MASTER
          I got stronger stuff. Homemade.

                    GRANT
          Thank you, no. Just a teetotaler.

                    STATION MASTER
          You got that in common with Mosby.

                    GRANT
          How so?

                    STATION MASTER
          He don't imbibe cups much neither.

                    GRANT
          Oh, we're much more alike than that.

                    STATION MASTER
          How's that, General?

                    GRANT
          We both know what it takes to win.

                    STATION MASTER
          What's that?

Grant takes a long puff and darts the stub into the ground.

GRANT
Never defend. Only attack your enemy.

EXT. TRAIN STATION - LATER

Mosby and his men return with prisoners, greeted by the Station Master.

STATION MASTER
Kinda' late to the party.

MOSBY
I'm listening.

STATION MASTER
Grant's on that train.

A black plume on the northern horizon gets smaller and smaller, and then a lonely WHISTLE lets loose.

MOSBY
Looks like he's staying on it too.

SAM CHAPMAN
Woulda' ended the war a sight quicker we tucked him under our belt.

MOSBY
Yeah, Grant's worth 50 Stoughtons.

SAM CHAPMAN
Better chance snatching old Abe outta' his bed.

MOSBY
What's that Sam?

SAM CHAPMAN
Grant's never alone. Ain't happening.

Sam trots off, but Mosby tracks the twisted soot.

MOSBY
I hear ya', Grumble. I hear ya'.

AARON (V.O.)
If we was fishing, Grant was just a throwback, considering what the Colonel hitched his mind to commence fishin' for next.

INT. CONFEDERATE WHITE HOUSE - EVENING

JEB parades in with Mosby and greets Lee, who chats with Mael de Fezints and PRESIDENT JEFFERSON DAVIS (57), a postage stamp look-a-like with goatee tuft and wavy gray hair.

                    LEE
Ah, General. Colonel Mosby. Allow me. Mister President, Mister Mael de Fezints, General JEB Stuart, and Colonel John Singleton Mosby.

                  JEFFERSON DAVIS
Gentlemen, welcome to Richmond.

Both officers half bow to Davis.

                  NOBLE TURPIN
Your exploits precede you both.

                  JEB STUART
The honor is mine, sir, to meet one who has given so much for our Cause.

                  NOBLE TURPIN
I fear we are all scarred by this conflict, General Stuart.

Mael de Fezints turns to shake Mosby's hand.

                  NOBLE TURPIN
Most are visible scars, but the worst wounds are deeper, and may go unseen.

                  MOSBY
I hope this plan may avert any further injuries, visible and otherwise.

                  JEFFERSON DAVIS
We can only hope Colonel, and we owe your idea our strongest consideration. Come, this way, gentlemen, please.

They approach the conference room doorway.

                  JEFFERSON DAVIS
I'd like you to meet our man in Washington, Mister John Wilkes Booth.

                  MOSBY
The actor?

JOHN WILKES BOOTH (26), spidery dark wisps shroud his coffin pale face. A brandy snifter hides a riverboat gambler's smile, and dull eyes that seem to probe each man's soul.

JOHN WILKES BOOTH
The actor? Sir, I am *the* actor.

INT. CONFERENCE ROOM

Booth, Mosby, Lee, and Jefferson Davis stand over a table where Mael de Fezints sits. JEB stares out the window.

JOHN WILKES BOOTH
I've watched him for months. Visits their hospital, the Soldier's Home, unguarded. That is our best chance.

NOBLE TURPIN
Always alone? And it's secluded?

JOHN WILKES BOOTH
Mostly, yes. Three miles from downtown, on a hill. No one around much. Easy to toss him in a buggy.

MOSBY
I like it. Multiple escape routes, near the Potomac, but no real fords. We may require a boat.

JOHN WILKES BOOTH
I have a man who knows the river.

JEB STUART
The Chesapeake's currents are maddening, especially at night.

JOHN WILKES BOOTH
He knows every eddy and swirl.

LEE
You think this feasible then, Colonel? We can get Lincoln here, to Richmond?

MOSBY
Drugged, at night, fresh riders every 10 miles. I think so. Just need to get across the river. I wonder, if there may not be an easier way.

JOHN WILKES BOOTH
Well, there is another way.

Everyone fixes on Booth.

JOHN WILKES BOOTH
Ah, uneasy lies the head that wears the crown.

Shrugs and glances all around.

                    JOHN WILKES BOOTH
Shakespeare. He walks at midnight. Some say he prays. I think his conscience preys upon him. An easy shot nonetheless.

                    MOSBY
That was not my meaning, Wilkes. I will have no part in that.

                    JEFFERSON DAVIS
Well, it certainly makes me wonder.

                    LEE
You would condone murder, a civilian?

                    JEFFERSON DAVIS
If we thought of it, who is watching where I go every day and having this same meeting, right now, with Lincoln?

EXT. NATIONAL HOTEL, WASHINGTON - NIGHT

A steady, freezing drizzle empties the downtown streets.

INT. BOOTH'S ROOM

A bottle, glasses, and maps clutter the kidnapper's table.

                    JOHN WILKES BOOTH
We exchange him for our POW's, or make them end the war straight up, or...we take it into our own hands.

                    WAT BOWIE
Kill him?

                    JOHN WILKES BOOTH
And his cabinet. Easy enough to get Vice President Johnson and Secretary of State Seward. We each take one.

                    WAT BOWIE
Cut the head off, snake dies.

                    JOHN WILKES BOOTH
He comes to my theater all the time. Everyone knows me. I could easily enter his box-

                    MOSBY
The plan is to take him alive.

                    WAT BOWIE
          Love to put my boot on his scrawny
          neck, them bones just a snappin'.

                    JOHN WILKES BOOTH
          You know Mosby, not one Southern
          mother would shed a tear for him.

                    WAT BOWIE
          Them darkies would flood the Potomac.

                    MOSBY
          A dead President Lincoln serves no
          purpose for ending the war.

                    JOHN WILKES BOOTH
          Begging for a bullet, if you ask me.

                    MOSBY
          No one did.

Booth takes a shot, pours another. Downs it and pours again.

                    MOSBY
          Any man unclear on our mission, I'm
          prepared to underscore it. <u>Now</u>.

Booth throws back his drink. An awkward silence settles.

                    WAT BOWIE
          Mister Booth, could I ask a favor,
          one Southern patriot to another?

                    JOHN WILKES BOOTH
          My unmitigated pleasure, sir. Ask
          and up to half my kingdom is yours.

                    WAT BOWIE
          Could I have...your autograph?

Smiles break the ice. Booth retrieves a card and scrawls.

                    JOHN WILKES BOOTH
          There you are. We few, we happy
          few, we band of brothers.

Wat studies the card and then screws up his face.

                    WAT BOWIE
          John B Wilkes?

Booth scratches it out, and signs again. A beaming Wat shows
Mosby, who is less impressed and eyes Booth.

                    JOHN WILKES BOOTH
          A stage name, ah, but what's in a
          name? Or a rose? I must be drunk.
          A drink? A toast to Lincoln's demise.

                    MOSBY
          I will toast his good health and a
          safe arrival in Richmond, alive.

EXT. WHITE HOUSE, FRONT PORCH - MORNING

MARY TODD LINCOLN (47), hands Lincoln his topcoat and hat.
Some folks thought in the past she may have been pretty.

                    LINCOLN
          Do not fret, Mary. I go for me, but
          they appreciate it too, I think.

                    MARY TODD LINCOLN
          If you must go, take that no good
          bodyguard. Always underfoot anyway.

                    LINCOLN
          It's in His hands, Mother. Not ours.

                    MARY TODD LINCOLN
          I am only asking you to put something
          else in God's hands, something He
          can use, Abraham. You worry me so.

He kisses her head and takes his horse from the black footman.

EXT. BRICK WAREHOUSE, OUTSIDE WASHINGTON - MORNING

Surrounded by forests and swamps, with a clear view of the
Soldiers Home intersection, sits a charred warehouse.

INT. SECOND FLOOR

Booth, Mosby, and Wat crouch at an upstairs window. Between
the two men, Wat rests a Sharps Carbine on the windowsill.

A lanky rider, with a stove pipe hat, lopes in the distance.

                    JOHN WILKES BOOTH
          Fame, the likes of Bobby Edward Lee.

                    MOSBY
          That will do. We're here to scout.

                    JOHN WILKES BOOTH
          The boy hero who won our independence.

                    MOSBY
          Enough Wilkes.

Wat's eyes shift sideways at Mosby, sweat beads form on his
upper lip, the gun still sighted down the street.

>   JOHN WILKES BOOTH
>   Maybe even a city...Bowie, Virginia.

Booth enjoys the banter, winks, but only gets a dark look.

>   MOSBY
>   Put the gun down, Wat.

>   JOHN WILKES BOOTH
>   Johnson is a slaveholding Tennessean.
>   He wants peace. Think of all the
>   men's lives you will save, both sides.

>   MOSBY
>   You bust that cap and all Hell comes
>   down on the South. Do not even think
>   about it, Wat. Johnson hates us.

>   JOHN WILKES BOOTH
>   Abe loves darkies, you know. Wants
>   them to vote. And marry...our women.

>   MOSBY
>   I am ordering you, Wat.

Wat's knuckle whitens on the trigger, and then Mosby slams
down the muzzle.

The shot startles them and Lincoln's hat flips. Mosby has
his Colt out and aimed at Booth's temple in half a heartbeat.

>   MOSBY
>   Sometimes I question your sanity.

>   JOHN WILKES BOOTH
>   The boy had a shot at glory is all.
>   No harm done, Colonel.

Soldiers and doctors rush out of the cottage, a crowd forms
around Lincoln's horse. Lincoln smooths his hair, accepts
his hat, and pokes a finger through the hole.

>   MOSBY
>   Best git.

Mosby jerks Wat up with him and throws him to the stairs.

We see Booth has a Derringer cocked under his jacket, pointed
at Mosby the whole time.

They both dash down the steps, but Booth stays and watches
the scene unfold below.

82.

JOHN WILKES BOOTH
Glory, like a circle in the water, which never ceaseth to enlarge itself, passes to the next man.

INT. LINCOLN'S OFFICE - MORNING

Grant and Lincoln, alone, sit close together.

LINCOLN
Much of our future has been lost, Mister Grant. Doctors, inventors. Men who may have bettered our lives. Thousands perhaps, forever gone.

GRANT
It's coming to an end, sir. Lee's men are coming through our lines every night, by the hundreds. It's just a matter of weeks, tops.

LINCOLN
My soul has ached for those words. Sleepless prayers finally heard.

GRANT
Most praying for them to hang, sir. Probably not enough hemp in Kentucky for stretching all them necks.

LINCOLN
To be sure, Lee and Davis are a national stain, but more blood will not scour it clean.

GRANT
And Mosby and his gang? How would you like it handled, once Lee's in the bag?

LINCOLN
Do you recollect the Bible story about Saint Paul's escape from Damascus? How he got away?

GRANT
Lowered over the wall in a basket, if memory serves.

LINCOLN
Know what his disciples said? Let 'em down easy. Let 'em down easy.

GRANT
I only look smart, Mister President.

                    LINCOLN
          That is what I would like to do,
          Mister Grant. We need to put the
          Union together, and we cannot hang
          their heroes and expect much support,
          now can we?

                    GRANT
          Folks are gonna' want some revenge.

                    LINCOLN
          But I do not. Let 'em down easy,
          Mister Grant. Besides, you may run
          for office some day. Rebel votes in
          your back pocket may be mighty handy.

                    GRANT
          No disrespect meant sir, but after
          seeing how this war wears on you,
          well, I'd sooner run <u>from</u> office.

                    LINCOLN
          That reminds me of a story. I knew
          a widow in Springfield, toted a two-
          legged cat on her shoulder, and she
          wanted to run for mayor, well....

INT. LEE'S TENT - EVENING

SUPER: LEE'S HQ, APPOMATTOX COURTHOUSE, VIRGINIA

Lee sits in a spartan tent, a cracker box table and one chair, trembling a letter near a lone candle stub.

INSERT - The letter reads:

"*General R.E. Lee, Commanding C.S.A.:*

                              5 P.M., April 7th, 1865.

The results of the last week must convince you of the hopelessness of further resistance on the part of the Army of Northern Virginia in this struggle. I feel that it is so, and regard it as my duty to shift from myself the responsibility of any further effusion of blood by asking of you the surrender of that portion of the Confederate States army known as the Army of Northern Virginia.

U.S. Grant, Lieutenant-General"

An officer's hand knocks on the tent pole before entering.

                    WALTER TAYLOR
          You wanted to see me, sir?

                    LEE
          Mister Taylor. I require my sword.

                    WALTER TAYLOR
          Sir?

                    LEE
          My sword. Do you know where it is?

                    WALTER TAYLOR
          You never wear a sword, sir.

                    LEE
          I must reply to Grant, and I fear,
          surrender this army tomorrow. I
          would rather die a thousand deaths,
          but I am afraid we are played out.

                    WALTER TAYLOR
          General Lee-

                    LEE
          Please, summon a courier and accompany
          him through the lines with my reply.
          I will have it for you shortly.

                    WALTER TAYLOR
          Sir, I...we can still, maybe a-

Lee shakes his silver head.

                    WALTER TAYLOR
          Will there be anything else, General?

                    LEE
          Please see that my sword is
          presentable, and my best uniform.
          Grant will own both tomorrow. I
          would like to look my very best.

                    WALTER TAYLOR
          Yes General. I will see to it myself,
          sir. And sir, it has been...an honor.

EXT. VIRGINIA COUNTRYSIDE - NIGHT

SUPER: NEAR LUD LAKE'S SAFEHOUSE

Mosby and Aaron combat an icy rain, losing badly. In the
distance a light flutters between veils of sleet.

                    AARON
          Looks like Mistuh Lud still up.

                    MOSBY
          Hear his wife still has real coffee.

                    AARON
          No Bluebirds out in this mess. Too
          raw. Hot coffee do a heap a good.

                    MOSBY
          Let us pay our respects, Aaron.

INT. DINNER

Mosby pushes away from the table, while ISRAEL (10), their
slave boy, clears dishes with MRS LAKE (45). Mosby stands.

                    MOSBY
          Ma'am, that was the finest ribs-

KAH-BLAM!

A shot bursts the window pane. Glass clatters to the floor,
along with Mosby, clutching his stomach.

                    LUD LAKE
          Lights! Anybody hit?

                    MOSBY
          I am...shot.

LUD (47), and his wife scramble to blow out the lanterns.

                    YANKEE TROOPER (O.S.)
          Hold on there, Zeb, you dang fool!

                    YANKEE TROOPER 2 (O.S.)
          Horse reared. Weren't me.

                    YANKEE TROOPER (O.S.)
          You folks okay in there? We're
          meaning no harm. Looking for Mosby.

Mosby writhes in pain, his head now in Aaron's lap.

                    LUD LAKE
               (whispering)
          Is'ral, out back, hitch up the cart.

Israel moves to the rear door.

                    MRS LAKE
          Keep him talking Is'ral. Do not let
          him pass out.

                    LUD LAKE
          Back trail through the woods to Widow
          Tapp's place. Right into the barn,
          then fetch her up. High-tail it!

                    ISRAEL
          Yes 'em. Keep 'im talkin'.

Aaron crams a napkin into Mosby's gut and presses it down.

                    AARON
          I come on directly, Colonel. Promise.

He helps Mosby to his feet and out the rear door.

EXT. VIRGINIA COUNTRYSIDE

A murderous downpour, ice, hail, and rain drench the boy,
his mule, and the cart with Mosby in the back, shivering
under soaked blankets and quilts.

                    ISRAEL
          Sorry Colonel. I's goin' fast as
          old Ethel allows in dis' mud. Cart
          ain't her usual get up. She used to
          runnin' free.

                    MOSBY
          We all are.

                    ISRAEL
          Mebbe you is. Can't even spell it.

Mosby tugs at the bloody quilt, nodding off.

                    MOSBY
          Spell?

                    ISRAEL
          Free. Can't spell it, but I sho'
          ain't got none, I know dat much.

                    MOSBY
          Lud's good folk. You're free enough.

                    ISRAEL
          Beggin' pardon, Colonel, but I been
          told to take you to Widow Tapp's
          place. No one asked me if I wanted
          to go. I ain't choosin' to go for
          this buggy ride on such a devil's
          night as this.

Mosby considers this, his head rolls, battling sleep.

                    ISRAEL
          Ain't free if you can't do what you
          want, when you want, how you want.

                    MOSBY
               (losing the fight)
          Freedom...is...falling off a log.

                    ISRAEL
          What's that, Colonel? You still
          with me, Colonel? Colonel!

Mosby is unconscious, his blankets soaked in rain and blood.

                    ISRAEL
          Even _told_ keep you talkin' sound
          like freedom? C'mon Ethel, git on
          with bein' free. Yaw!

INT. SECRET SERVICE OFFICE, RICHMOND - MORNING

Mael de Fezints smacks his cane on the table.

                    NOBLE TURPIN
          How are we supposed to get Lincoln
          out if I do not know where Mosby is?
          He planned the confounded route!

                    WAT BOWIE
          I am sorry, sir. None of us know
          where he is, except maybe Sam, and
          he ain't saying.

                    NOBLE TURPIN
          I _must_ talk to him!

                    WAT BOWIE
          It's his way, for protection, and
          ours. All I know is he's hurt bad.

                    NOBLE TURPIN
          What about his darkie?

                    WAT BOWIE
          He's with him too. Can't say more.

                    NOBLE TURPIN
          Fine, we'll just ask Grant to hold
          off while we get our damn ducks in a
          row to kidnap his President? Get
          out of my sight!

EXT. TAVERN, OUTSIDE WASHINGTON - NIGHT

SUPER: SURRATT'S TAVERN, MARYLAND

Middle of nothing farmhouse, posing as a tavern, squats on two forsaken roads. A tired stable shares its sentence.

INT. BARROOM

Smoky whispers and drunken banter fill a low ceiling dirt floored basement. Mael de Fezints perches in the darkest corner with Booth.

              JOHN WILKES BOOTH
     Why not New York, then Canada?

              NOBLE TURPIN
     If you make it out of Washington, I
     will be most impressed, Wilkes.

              JOHN WILKES BOOTH
     You underestimate me, Mael de Fezints.
     Have you never heard the actors'
     creed? The show must go on!

              NOBLE TURPIN
     So long as Mosby shows, that is all
     the show I need.

              JOHN WILKES BOOTH
     And my man will deliver him right to
     you. Should be quite an encore.

EXT. LEE'S CAMP - EVENING

A listless camp where a few men sit or go through the motions.

A COURIER (24), charges into the camp, hooves shatter the mournful lull, steam and moonlight mix over his lathered steed, as he slide-stops at the main tent.

The men return to their fires, unmoved, mindlessly poking the dying embers with a pallbearer's trance.

              COURIER
     I have an urgent message from Richmond
     for General Lee!

Walter Taylor looks up, sighs, and steps out of the tent.

              WALTER TAYLOR
     Son, ain't nothing urgent here.

Disinterested, he reaches up, as he's done a thousand times.

              COURIER
     Begging your pardon, sir, but I'm to
     confirm the message is placed in
     General Lee's hand. Orders.

                    WALTER TAYLOR
          Uh, huh. Orders, eh? This way.

He dismounts and follows Taylor to a distant campfire. Lee
slumps, head in hand, his uniform's rank insignia removed.
Two Rebs cross their rifles as they approach his refuge.

                    WALTER TAYLOR
          The General does not wish to be
          disturbed tonight. Orders. You may
          watch me give it to him.

The courier moves the envelope away from Taylor's hand.

                    WALTER TAYLOR
          Or take it back to Richmond. Either
          way, we don't much give a damn anymore
          about Richmond's orders.

After a moment, he relents, and hands over the message.

EXT. NEAR LEE'S CAMP - LATER

A pack, led by Lee, rides up to a mill on Muddy Creek.
Another rider, Walter Taylor, approaches at a brisk pace.

                    WALTER TAYLOR
          On his way, sir. Just behind me.
          He's wounded, mighty slow going.

                    LEE
          His only fault. He keeps getting
          shot. Very well, Mister Taylor.

                    WALTER TAYLOR
          I believe that is them now, sir.

Lee rides forward. Wat, Powell, Aaron, and Mosby stop.

                    LEE
          A word with your Colonel, gentlemen?

The men can only stare, manage a salute, and then move off.

                    LEE
          I've lost count. Your fourth wound?

                    MOSBY
          My heart is wounded more after hearing
          your news. How are you, sir?

                    LEE
          What's done is done, up to the
          Almighty now. And Grant. Some think
          they are one in the same.

Both chuckle, but far from a real laugh.

LEE
We are dispersed, Colonel. The Army of Northern Virginia has done its duty and my men are heading home. Sadly, far too many never shall.

MOSBY
Yes, sir. Some mighty sad days ahead.

LEE
Perhaps more than you realize. We seem to have a more dire situation. I received this from Mael de Fezints.

He hands the message to Mosby.

LEE
I fear our surrender has made Richmond mad with desperation. You are the only man close enough to Booth to know where he may strike, and that I trust can get himself into Washington.

Mosby studies the paper.

LEE
The theater is Mael de Fezint's feeling on the matter. Tonight.

MOSBY
Tonight? You're ordering me to go up against our own government?

LEE
Colonel, may I remind you, we have been doing precisely that for nigh-on five years now. And I am asking.

MOSBY
But sir, Lincoln? Our country-

LEE
Our country of independent states no longer exists, as we knew it.

MOSBY
But Virginia is always first.

LEE
No more, sir. No more. Before the War we said, these United States of America *are*. From now on we will say the United States of America *is*.

He nods at Aaron, alone, abandoned by Powell and Wat.

> LEE
> His future, and ours, will be best served by Mister Lincoln, who General Grant has just informed me wishes to "let the South down easy." All of our futures are tied to Lincoln.

> MOSBY
> I know Johnson. A friend of the family, of sorts. We will not fare well with him as President.

> LEE
> Indeed. Such is my individual way of thinking. Vice President Johnson is no friend to the South, black or white. Without Lincoln, we will lose more than a war. Perhaps all.

> MOSBY
> And killing a civilian, when the war is all but over, is illegal, unethical by any code of modern warfare.

> LEE
> To be clear, sir, and make no mistake, it is murder in the eyes of God.

> MOSBY
> It's insanity. Our cause is lost.

> LEE
> Indeed. Indeed it is.

They pause and take in the depth of their words.

> LEE
> Pray tell, can you stop him? Our reclamation may be at stake for generations.

> MOSBY
> I cannot ride all the way to Washington, but I have a man who knows Booth and his haunts. If he can find him, but....

> LEE
> Do go on, sir, I pray you. Time is of the essence.

                    MOSBY
          General, I'm just not sure he wouldn't
          pull the trigger himself.

                    LEE
          Not a Republican, eh? Maybe send a
          second man to make sure he understands
          the severity of our situation. A
          man you trust better.

                    MOSBY
          Yes, Powell does know Washington,
          but I'd prefer one of my officers.

                    LEE
          I have learned that if we cannot do
          what we prefer, we must do what we
          can. A hard lesson thrust upon me
          these last few weeks. They must do.

EXT.   OUTSIDE LEE'S CAMP - LATER

Powell and Wat mount, and turn to face a standing Mosby.

                    LEWIS POWELL
          You sure, Colonel? We can ride easy.

                    MOSBY
          Only slow you down. Remember, if
          not the theater, then his saloon.

Wat and Powell nod and move off. Mosby returns to Aaron and
the horses, and sees something hanging from a bedroll.

                    AARON
          They make better time with our horses.

                    MOSBY
          Is that Wat's horse?

                    AARON
          Not for certain which is which, sir.

Mosby tugs on it. A leather courier tube slides out of the
blanket roll. Mosby opens it and retrieves a paper.

INSERT - A letter, in code, signed *John B Wilkes*!

                    AARON
          What's it say, Colonel?

Mosby glances back at the two men galloping away.

                    MOSBY
          Says we're going to Washington.

EXT. WASHINGTON OUTSKIRTS - NIGHT

Powell and Wat canter over the Navy Yard Bridge, the completed Capitol Dome in the distance, lit up by a fireworks spray.

EXT. LINCOLN'S CARRIAGE

The Lincolns ride in an open carriage facing the Dome, MAJOR RATHBONE (27), and his fiancee', CLARA HARRIS (31).

> LINCOLN
> Lee and the Capitol Dome, both finished. Very good omens.

> MAJOR RATHBONE
> My true love at my side, and a night at the theater with the President and his bride. Also good omens.

They come to a stop in front of Ford's Theater where a small crowd cheers their arrival.

> LINCOLN
> It does my old heart good to see young lovers in April. Hope springs eternal, remember Mother?

Lincoln winks at her, then waves to the well-wishers and doffs his hat.

> LINCOLN
> How we were? It's never too late.

Mrs Lincoln gives him a disapproving look as she stands up.

> MARY TODD LINCOLN
> Despite being late, we do hope it is a special evening for both of you.

> CLARA HARRIS
> Thank you for inviting us. We'll always remember this night fondly.

Their black footman opens the door and helps Mrs Lincoln.

EXT. WASHINGTON - NIGHT

GUN SHOTS, FIRECRACKERS, ROCKETS, BANDS. The city throbs with revelers celebrating Grant's victory over Lee.

EXT. FORD'S THEATER

The two Rangers ride past Ford's Theater and stop at the alley. Some SOLDIERS in front of the tavern next door, singing and laughing, stumble toward the alley.

                    DRUNKEN SERGEANT
          You two. What're you two up to there?

                    WAT BOWIE
          Just looking for the stable.

                    DRUNKEN SERGEANT
          You talk like Rebs. Where you from?

                    WAT BOWIE
          Port Tobacco, the Union side of the
          river. Can't seem to shake my drawl.

                    DRUNKEN SERGEANT
          Back of the theater, down the alley.

                    LEWIS POWELL
          Much obliged.

                    DRUNKEN SERGEANT
          Hurrah for Abe! Hurrah for Grant!

                    LEWIS POWELL
          Right, hurrah for our great generals.

The pair trot down the alley, dismount, and tie their horses
at the livery stable's corner, near Ford's rear entrance.

                    WAT BOWIE
          Take the back door, his room's on
          the right. I'll check the tavern.

                    LEWIS POWELL
          Fifteen minutes, meet at the box?

                    WAT BOWIE
          But no shooting.

Powell pulls back his coat and reveals a massive Bowie knife.

They both check their pocket watches and separate. Powell
begins to leave, stops, and makes sure Wat turns the corner
to the street, then slinks up to the stage door.

EXT. FRONT

The drunken soldiers sway toward Wat, motioning to join them,
so he turns away and goes into Ford's Theater instead.

INT. INSIDE

The HEAD USHER (45), turns to greet Wat.

                    HEAD USHER
          Running late, sir?

                    WAT BOWIE
          Uh, yes. Some crowd.

                    HEAD USHER
          The President always packs the house.

                    WAT BOWIE
          Lincoln's here then?

                    HEAD USHER
          Upstairs. In his box. Creates quite
          a stir, plenty of headaches though.
          Your ticket?

                    WAT BOWIE
          Oh yes. Let me see now.

Another usher, frantic, waves the Head Usher toward him.

                    HEAD USHER
          As I said. Please excuse me, sir.

Both ushers move off. Wat sprints up the main stairway.

EXT. FRONT

Mosby and Aaron arrive. The soldiers next door, still singing and drinking, stumble from the alley corner toward some women.

                    MOSBY
          I'll wait here. Go on to the stage
          door. See if you can see them.

                    AARON
          You lookin' peaked, Colonel. Mebbe
          we best get you back to bed-

                    MOSBY
          I'm fine. Go check, then signal me.

Aaron trots into the ink, while Mosby waits. He pulls back his cloak. Fresh blood sops his shirt.

INT. REAR

Powell listens to the PLAY for a moment, goes to the dressing room hallway, and tries the first doorknob. It turns freely.

EXT. FRONT

Mosby turns the corner and clops into the alley, and as he does, a lavish ebony coach rolls up, a saddled horse in tow.

INT. HALLWAY

Powell presses the dressing room door a crack and sees a seated Booth, his back to Powell, primping in the mirror.

INT. ALLEY

Mosby tries to ride, gives it up, and cringes in his dismount.

INT. BOOTH'S DRESSING ROOM

Powell, cat-like, knife in hand, within striking distance.

Booth spins around, a pistol leveled at Powell's crotch.

          JOHN WILKES BOOTH
   Been expecting you.

INT. UPSTAIRS

Wat walks behind the last row, toward the private box hallway. He rounds the bend and sees LINCOLN'S BODYGUARD (38).

          LINCOLN'S BODYGUARD
   That'll do. No admittance past here.

          WAT BOWIE
   I...I seem to have lost my wife.
   Have you seen a tall woman in a black-

          LINCOLN'S BODYGUARD
   Your finger.

Wat looks at his hands.

          LINCOLN'S BODYGUARD
   No wedding ring.

INT. BOOTH'S DRESSING ROOM

Booth sneers the "cat-eating-shit-grin" and stands up. Powell lowers his knife and...the two men embrace!

          LEWIS POWELL
   You should be more careful, Wilkes.

          JOHN WILKES BOOTH
   No one suspects me. I'm the star.

          LEWIS POWELL
   Then he's really here?

Booth nods, stows the pistol, and hands Powell the package.

                    JOHN WILKES BOOTH
          And Mosby?

                    LEWIS POWELL
          Soon enough, unless he's blind.
          Even his cook can't miss that clue.

                    JOHN WILKES BOOTH
          Here's the medicine. Seward is
          confined to bed, top floor. I'll
          see you at Surratt's. Avenge Lee!

Powell takes the small box, beams, and hurries off. Booth
checks his watch and slips out in the opposite direction.

EXT. ALLEY

Aaron approaches the stage door, but NED SPANGLER (40),
notices and stops him.

                    NED SPANGLER
          Whoa, where you going, Buck? You
          ain't allowed. Come on over here.

Aaron sighs and does what he's told.

EXT. ALLEY - MOMENTS LATER

Mosby strains up the corridor, leans against his horse for
support, as Powell exits the front of the theater.

Powell acknowledges the carriage with a head bob, unties the
horse, and rides away.

The carriage turns into the alley, passes Mosby, and stops
near the far end. A man gets out, unseen in the murk, and
moves against the alley wall.

The carriage rolls on into the livery stable.

Mosby approaches, clutching his side. He stops and ties off
his horse near the livery stable corner.

                    NOBLE TURPIN
          Put your hands up and turn around.

Mosby obeys, but he can only lift one arm, wincing.

                    MOSBY
          I'm wounded. I have no money.

                    NOBLE TURPIN
          This is not a 'money or your life'
          proposition. Just life, Mosby.

Turpin steps into the light, with a pepperbox pistol.

                    MOSBY
          Mael de Fezints?

                    NOBLE TURPIN
          Look closer. You know me much better.

He drops his mask. Mosby turns from the scrambled features.

                    NOBLE TURPIN
          Surely you can see the family
          resemblance...to George.

                    MOSBY
          George?

Turpin cranes closer, but Mosby steps back to the corner.

                    MOSBY
          Turpin!

INT. OUTSIDE PRESIDENT'S BOX - MOMENTS LATER

Wat hides his hand.

Lincoln's bodyguard reaches for a pistol. Wat springs, shoves him backward over his chair and dashes past.

Lincoln's bodyguard gets up, stops, and looks back at the President's head. He hesitates, then chases after Wat.

EXT. ALLEY

Turpin canes closer.

                    MOSBY
          But Manassas? You're dead.

                    NOBLE TURPIN
          Inside maybe, or a ghost, like you.

                    MOSBY
          I'm nothing like you.

                    NOBLE TURPIN
          Not Lee's Gray Ghost anymore? I
          knew if I told him, he'd send you.

                    MOSBY
          You're behind all this? It'll crush
          the South. They'll forgive a lot,
          but never murdering their President.

                    NOBLE TURPIN
          Such an ugly word. Father Abraham
          deserves better. The President should
          be...assassinated. Much more
          dignified. Just another casualty of
          war. Now Absalom, that was murder.

                    MOSBY
          I knew it! You sick puke. Why hurt
          a boy? A poor boy!

Mosby stops backing up, but the pistol flicks his advance.

                    NOBLE TURPIN
          Hard to reach you in jail, but I
          could reach what you loved. Not
          nearly as satisfying as this is going
          to be, but I enjoyed your pain.

The muzzle shoves a weakened Mosby backward.

                    NOBLE TURPIN
          You know I stood outside your cell
          window that night, listened to you
          cry. Quite refreshing.

He pokes him again, clearly enjoying the cat and mouse game.

                    MOSBY
          You won't get away with this.

                    NOBLE TURPIN
          Oh, but I will because they will
          find your body here in the alley,
          with your gun, and a suicide note.

He pats his vest pocket.

                    NOBLE TURPIN
          The great Mosby, killed after shooting
          the President. History will not be
          kind. Raving lunatic, sick over
          Lee's surrender, snaps and shoots
          Lincoln. Nice headline.

INT. UPSTAIRS VERANDA

Wat darts into a doorway and finds himself

OUTSIDE ABOVE THE ALLEY

A rickety catwalk, to the bar next door, sags before Wat.

Lincoln's bodyguard rushes from behind, pistol drawn.

EXT. ALLEY

                    MOSBY
          You're mad as a hatter. All this,
          and killing a boy, for what?

                    NOBLE TURPIN
          Revenge seems trite. How 'bout
          justice? Gives you a sense what's
          been sittin' in my craw all these
          years. Now your own gun here, is
          gonna tear your throat out just like
          you done to George.

Turpin trains the gun.

                    NOBLE TURPIN
          Poetic justice, eh? Open wide.

Mosby staggers back.

Past the stable corner.

Drops to one knee, drained.

ABOVE

Lincoln's bodyguard shoots!

Wat crashes through the far door.

BELOW

Turpin looks up.

From around the corner a pitchfork thrusts!

Tines burst through Turpin's neck!

                    AARON
          Swallow this, you egg suckin' bastard!

A twist and jerk! Turpin's head toggles, his neck snaps.

Turpin slumps to his knees.

Eye to eye with Mosby, shocked, head limp.

He gurgles bloody spurts.

And oozes to the ground.

Mosby grabs his gun and the suicide note.

ABOVE

A SCREAM curdles the night air!

Lincoln's bodyguard bolts back inside.

INT. PRESIDENTIAL BOX - CONTINUOUS

A blue smoke cloud reveals:

CHAOS

Booth slashes and stabs Rathbone over the slumped Lincoln.

Mary screams again, and then Clara screams.

Booth leaps the half-wall and flops hard onto the stage below!

He thrusts the knife over his head.

              JOHN WILKES BOOTH
     Sic Semper Tyrannis!

Booth shuffles offstage, dragging his left foot, hopping. A swipe at a stunned actor clears his way to the alley door.

              MARY TODD LINCOLN
     A doctor! The President is shot!

THE AUDIENCE

As it registers, screams and shouts fill the room!

PANDEMONIUM!

Men charge onto the stage, wooden chairs tossed, orders yelled, appeals for doctors, soldiers rush to the Presidential Box, hoisting themselves up from the stage.

EXT. LAFAYETTE SQUARE, WASHINGTON - CONTINUOUS

SUPER: SECRETARY OF STATE SEWARD'S HOME

A three story brick mansion, lit up by multiple SCREAMS.

INT. BEDROOM

Darkness, like a stack of black cats.

Powell straddles WILLIAM SEWARD (63), driving his knife into the squirming bed sheets.

Blood SPLASHES against the wall.

Frantic nurses wrestle him to the floor, SCREAMS for help!

                    LEWIS POWELL
               I am mad, mad, mad!

He flies from the room, blood drenched, in a demonic fury.

EXT. ALLEY - MOMENTS LATER

Booth gallops past Mosby and Aaron, his horse leaps Turpin's body, the pitchfork wags as the horse's belly grazes it.

                    MOSBY
               Booth! Booth!

                    JOHN WILKES BOOTH
               Glory, Mosby! Glory hallelujah!
               The South is avenged!

Aaron helps Mosby to his feet.

                    AARON
               Can you ride, Mistuh John?

                    MOSBY
               Just get me in the saddle.

Aaron struggles to help him to his horse.

Wat, mounted, appears at the end of the alley, waving.

The three men thunder into the night. HYSTERICAL SHOUTS fill the darkness behind them.

EXT. OUTSKIRTS SMALL TOWN - EARLY MORNING

SUPER: SALEM, VIRGINIA, APRIL 21, 1865

A brutal fog engulfs a mounted Mosby. He faces 200 misty Rangers, lined up in a crisp parade formation.

                    MOSBY (V.O.)
               "My Dearest Pauline. I will be home
               soon, as I am sure you have heard
               the news. I long to see you and,
               although no words can match my aching
               heart, I do derive some comfort in
               the thought of you in my arms in but
               a few days.

Sam Chapman trots forward, tears stream down his face.

                    MOSBY (V.O.)
          "This joy is compounded by the sorrow
          of disbanding the 43rd. I can no
          longer fight, but I cannot bring
          myself to admit defeat, and refuse
          to surrender my men.

Aaron, in the background, sits on his horse.

                    MOSBY (V.O.)
          "You asked of Aaron, but I cannot
          say what he will do...

Sam looks back at Mosby who nods reassuringly.

                    SAM CHAPMAN
                (choking tears)

"Soldiers!

I have summoned you together for the last time. The vision we cherished of a free and independent country has vanished and that country is now the spoil of a conqueror.

I disband your organization in preference to our surrendering it to our enemies. I am no longer your commander. After an association of more than two eventful years. I part from you with a just pride in the fame of your achievements and grateful recollections of your generous kindness to myself.

And now, at this moment of bidding you a final adieu, accept his assurance of my unchanging confidence & regard.

Farewell!"

Mosby shakes the hand of every single man, tears and hugs flow like the mighty Shenandoah.

When the last Ranger has ridden off, Mosby approaches Aaron.

                    MOSBY
          This may be a fool's question, on
          today of all days, but, are you happy?

                    AARON
          Well sir, not for your loss today,
          course. Feel mighty poorly for you.

                    MOSBY
          No, I mean are _you_ happy, with how
          I've treated you?

                    AARON
          You askin' if I'd done it how you
          done it, cotton to all this fightin'?

                    MOSBY
          I fought for independence, but at
          your expense. I see that now. But,
          I don't get it, why you stayed.

                    AARON
          Well sir, strike me funny you askin'
          after all this time. Seemed plain,
          like the back of my hand.

He holds up his hand and shows Absalom's nail ring.

                    AARON
          You think I had to stay? No sir, I
          done it cuz I <u>chose</u> to stay, Colonel.

                    MOSBY
          But why?

                    AARON
          To protect you, keep you from harm.
          I wanted to serve you, Colonel, cuz
          we friends, just like how you and
          Abby was. Figgered that's how he'd
          do it if he was here, so I just done
          it for him. I stayed for you.

Mosby is stunned and cannot speak for a moment.

                    AARON
          Ain't that what you and Abby was,
          Colonel? Friends for life.

Mosby nods and just stares into Aaron's eyes for a bit.

                    MOSBY
          I want you to have this, before I
          officially give up, so you know I
          would have done it, win or lose.

He hands Aaron the gilded envelope he received on his wedding
day. We see words on it that were not there when Alfred
gave it to him.

                    AARON
          You knows I don't know my letters.

                    MOSBY
          It says, "Whenever I hear anyone
          arguing for slavery, I feel a strong
          impulse to have it tried on him."

Aaron shakes his head, not grasping.

                    MOSBY
          I am setting you free. Before they
          make us do it, I want you to know,
          in my heart, you were always a free
          man to me, old friend.

He moves his fingertips over the words.

                    AARON
          Friend.

Aaron chews on it. Tears rolling.

                    MOSBY (V.O.)
          "...because Aaron has not decided
          where he wants to go just yet. Your
          loving husband, John."

                    AARON
          Has a golden tinkle to these tired
          old ears.

                    MOSBY
          Overdue, I'm afraid. And there's
          500 Yankee greenbacks in there too.

Aaron looks up to the sky and closes his eyes.

                    MOSBY
          Mess a birthdays piled up on me.
          Sorry never gave them much mind.

                    AARON
          Them's good words to go with all
          that paper money. Who said 'em?

                    MOSBY
          Abraham Lincoln.

                    AARON
          That's real fine. Well sir, free so
          I do as I please then?

                    MOSBY
          That's right. Whatever you choose.

                    AARON
          Well sir, here's my first act as a
          free man. What Abby woulda' done.

He grabs Mosby and hugs him with all he has. Both men cry,
then laugh, and cry some more.

As they stroll, the fog parts.

MOSBY
I will always be your friend, Aaron.
One for all.

AARON
And all for one!

AARON (V.O.)
Colonel's heart busted that day.
Cried like a baby. All us Rangers
did, but in the end I got free.
Think mebbe the Colonel got freed up
some too, but the good Lord sheared
us down awful deep.

The cloud swirls behind the two men and then smothers them like ghostly apparitions fading into history.

AARON (V.O.)
Bible say all things work together
for good. Ain't thinning His words
none, but so much dying, them boys
cold in the ground, mostly dirt now,
hard pressed digging out much good.

The gray mist thickens, then turns over upon itself.

AARON (V.O.)
Some say Lord evened up the white
folk's sin on us colored. Maybe so.
Seem to me, leveled proper, a heap
more good needs wringing out yet.
No sir, make any sense that mess He
almost have to save the whole world.

EXT. SNOWY COUNTRY ROAD - MORNING

SUPER: SOUTH OF BASTOGNE, BELGIUM, DECEMBER, 1944

A fog bank exposes a man standing in a jeep that jerks to a stop at a fractured farmhouse. It is GENERAL PATTON (59).

Riding breeches and boots, a precision pressed uniform, and a searing scowl at a passing truck convoy, all underneath a lacquered three-star helmet. Some men are larger than life.

Behind him, several BLACK SOLDIERS unload gasoline drums for his tanks from a truck, a 12-inch red circle on the grill announces it as the famed *Red Ball Express*.

GENERAL HOBART GAY (50), a soldier's soldier without pretense or rank intimidation, ambushes Patton.

GENERAL GAY
Georgie! Please tell me it's a rumor.

PATTON
          Too damn slow, Hap, but we got no
          choice. Gas or no gas, we go tonight.

                    GENERAL GAY
          Spin the Third Army on a dime, on
          icy roads, and march 30 miles north,
          in this weather, into Model's five
          armored divisions? Your men are
          exhausted. It's not possible!

                    PATTON
          Precisely why it will work. Audacity,
          Hap. Always audacity. My men know
          there's Americans fighting for their
          lives in Bastogne, right now. On
          Christmas damn day! Turkey doesn't
          sit well when your buddies are dying.

Gay shakes his head and tries to speak.

                    PATTON
          You know what McAuliffe told them
          Nazi sumsabitches? He told 'em,
          "Nuts!" Man that won't surrender
          when he's beat needs a real Christmas
          present, Hap. I'm just playing Santa.

Patton hops down. His valet, GEORGE MEEKS (26), a black
sergeant, hands him his revolvers...ivory handled revolvers.

                    GENERAL GAY
          But Georgie, on Christmas day? The
          men need a rest.

Patton lifts his arms so Meeks can strap on his gunbelt.

                    PATTON
          Thank you, George. See these, Hap?

He strikes a gunfighter draw pose with both hands, pointing
down at the Colts while Meeks works.

                    PATTON
          Colonel John Mosby gave me these
          when I was a boy, told me fear is a
          weapon. Never forgot it. Been
          teaching his lesson all across Europe.

Meeks finishes and Patton drops his hands onto the handles.

PATTON
You hit a bully hard and fast, and
he'll run. Them no good Nazi bastards
are the biggest bullies I know and
we're gonna grab 'em by their nose
and kick their ass for killing
Americans on Christ's birthday!

He adjusts his gun belt, pats the handles, and sneers.

PATTON
Now. To beat a bully, especially if
he's bigger, you sock him right in
the nose, hard and fast. Hit 'em
first, and fear'll chew his ass
instead of yours.

Gay opens his mouth again, but Patton holds up his hand.

PATTON
Sorry, Hap. History lesson's over.
Time for them Nazi Huns to get some
Confederate schooling from Mosby!

Patton mounts a tank, and yells inside the turret.

PATTON
Lovely weather for killing Germans,
eh boys? Now, drive like <u>Hell</u> and I
promise not to <u>shit</u> in your tank!

Gay salutes Patton, who winks and returns it, as the tank column rumbles away. Scratching his head, Gay walks off.

A BLACK SOLDIER loads a drum onto another truck and then shuffles up to Sgt Meeks, an exaggerated dragging motion.

BLACK SOLDIER
Dat be alls you be needin', Massah
Patton, suh? Make me <u>sick</u>, waitin'
on that white old man, like some 'ol
field hand. Just a damn Uncle Tom!

Meeks continues to watch the tank column, unmoved, focused on Patton who winks and gives him a salute with his crop.

BLACK SOLDIER
You deaf and dumb, boy? Huh?

GEORGE MEEKS
In the Old Testament, a former slave
could choose to be a bondservant-

BLACK SOLDIER
Old Testament, like David and Goliath?

                          GEORGE MEEKS
                 Well sir, yes, just like that.

George bellies up and looks him smack in the eye.

                          GEORGE MEEKS
                 A freed slave would allow his ear to
                 be nailed to his master's door post
                 to signify that he freely chose to
                 serve him. A man could choose to be
                 a servant out of love for his master,
                 no matter the cause or sacrifice, he
                 served him out of love, no matter.

                          BLACK SOLDIER
                 You telling me you wait on him cuz
                 you want to? You choose to? Man,
                 next you be telling me you got your
                 ears pierced.

The black soldier shakes his head and continues loading drums.

                          GEORGE MEEKS
                      (to himself)
                 No. Only one ear.

We can see he does have a tiny stud, almost imperceptible,
in his ear. And then Meeks salutes in Patton's direction.
More swirling gray fog moves over the scene.

WHITE WORDS ON A BLACK SCREEN

General George "Georgie" Patton took Mosby's words to heart
and used the Philistine Philosophy to defeat the biggest
bully of the 20th century with speed and daring offensives.

Mosby continued to send checks to Aaron into his old age,
even when Mosby was nearly destitute. He died in 1916.

Secretary of State Seward recovered. Booth was shot and
killed less than two weeks later. Lewis Powell was hanged
on July 7th, 1865 with three other assassination accomplices.

Mosby's "Relative Superiority Tactics" are still taught at
West Point today, as the champion of the U.S. Army Rangers.

Exactly one year later, Sgt. George Meeks served as a
pallbearer at Patton's funeral...the only black soldier to
do so.

VINTAGE FILM OF PATTON'S FUNERAL IN LUXEMBURG WITH SGT. MEEKS

                            THE END

Made in the USA
Lexington, KY
14 July 2016